Being Unstoppable

BEING
UNSTOPPABLE

Conquering Your Everest

Seven Summits to Success

SEAN SWARNER

NEW YORK

LONDON • NASHVILLE • MELBOURNE • VANCOUVER

Being Unstoppable

Conquering Your Everest

© 2022 Sean Swarner

Published in New York, New York, by Morgan James Publishing. Morgan James is a trademark of Morgan James, LLC. www.MorganJamesPublishing.com

Morgan James BOGO™

A **FREE** ebook edition is available for you or a friend with the purchase of this print book.

_____

CLEARLY SIGN YOUR NAME ABOVE

Instructions to claim your free ebook edition:
1. Visit MorganJamesBOGO.com
2. Sign your name CLEARLY in the space above
3. Complete the form and submit a photo of this entire page
4. You or your friend can download the ebook to your preferred device

ISBN 9781631954382 paperback
ISBN 9781631954399 ebook
Library of Congress Control Number:
2020950778

Cover & Interior Design by:
Christopher Kirk
www.GFSstudio.com

Morgan James is a proud partner of Habitat for Humanity Peninsula and Greater Williamsburg. Partners in building since 2006.

Get involved today! Visit
MorganJamesPublishing.com/giving-back

Table of Contents

Acknowledgments

Sean's

First and foremost, there are *way* too many people to thank for supporting me, from public relations to media to sponsorship to people I've met during my travels who inspired me to a friend who saved my life on Denali (we'll get to that book soon), so I'll just keep it short.

My family (Mom, Dad, and Seth). Obviously, if it wasn't for my mom and dad, I wouldn't be alive, but I also wouldn't have been instilled with the desire to better myself every day. Also, thank you for encouraging me to take chances, and not be afraid. Seth, I mention you throughout the book, and you were an integral part to making my life-journey happen. I can't thank you enough.

My buddies from college: Brenda, Pat, Maurer, and Lupe. Thanks for the book, the CD, the fun memories, and for letting me win "the bet."

Marmot, you make the best outdoor gear on the planet. Rudy Project, you have saved my eyes countless times from the destruction of the sun. Leki, your poles have literally saved my life before. Innovative Skincare, your belief in me has been fantastic. And Morgan James Publishing, thanks for helping me share my story . . . let's change the world.

Last but definitely not least . . . every single person on Earth touched by cancer. You are the motivating factor in my life, and I hope I inspire you to do great things in your lives. Thank you for inspiring me to *Keep Climbing* and to *Live an Unstoppable Life*!

Lance's

First and above all, God. Thank you for leading me down this path.

Sonya Snow, my amazing wife. Thank you for being my biggest supporter and sharing me with this ambitious project as well as lending me your expertise in proofreading and being my guinea pig and sounding board for many of the steps and exercises in this book. Tyler, Logan, Conner and Hayley, thank you for being my motivation and thank you for sharing daddy with this project too. Thank you to my parents for raising me with ambition and cultivating my creativity.

Jim Trunzo, thank you for allowing me some of your time to learn from you...again. Who would have thought that even more than twenty years later I would still be learning from the best teacher I ever had in school. Thank you for your generosity.

James Woosley, thank you not only for your formatting services and working with us on our timeline, but also for answering many questions and providing me with guidance on getting this project off the ground. Also, your own books were a great influence on me.

Rob O'Friel, thank you for taking the time to sit down with me and sharing your experiences as a life coach. Those conversations were the beginning of this particular journey for me. For that time I am grateful.

Christopher Dixon, thank you for sharing your knowledge of ebooks, literature, and library systems with me as we kicked back on recliners over the holidays. Your feedback was a huge help in this endeavor.

Thank you to all of my Get Out Together followers, supporters, and guests. Thank you to my friends at Toastmasters for being a significant part of my personal development over the years. Thank you to Kevin Miller and the former professors and former members of good ol' Free Agent Academy, which changed my life.

Introduction

We should not worry about dying.
We should worry about not living
a life that matters.
—Sean Swarner

D o you have a goal you can't stop thinking about? Do
you have a dream you are yearning to chase, but just
don't know how to make it a reality? Do you keep putting it off until "someday?"

"Someday" is today. The world is ready for you to begin
your own journey to success and achieve your dream.

This book contains a story of one man's journey to accomplish what was once thought impossible. Sean overcame two
different cancers to make his dream of climbing Mt. Everest
(with one lung), the highest mountain in the world, a reality.

In addition to sharing his story with the world, Sean shares
the guiding principles that made his own dreams a reality.

This book begins with Sean's story of survival, adventure, and cliff-hanging suspense, and concludes with a section containing simple, practical steps you can use to fulfill your own dream and goals. You'll learn how Sean managed to make the impossible possible, and incorporate those same, simple, but powerful steps into climbing your own Everest.

This is the first of a series of books, where each one chronicles Sean's story on a different mountain throughout his quest to climb the famed Seven Summits (the highest mountain on each of the seven continents). Each book concludes with different guiding principles, practical, easy steps, and exercises. Each book will help you create critical life-changing habits, and build upon those from each preceding book. If they worked for Sean to make history, and accomplish the "impossible," we have no doubt they'll change your life and help you live the life you have always dreamed of.

Let the journey begin!

—Lance Snow

PART I
Fighting for My Life

By Sean Swarner

Chapter 1

*The journey of a thousand miles
begins with one step.*
—Lao Tsu

I just spent nearly a month and a half on an ice-covered
mountain, climbing up and down countless times in order
to establish different camps and get my body used to the
extreme altitude. Wrapped up in my negative-forty-degree
sleeping bag, I lay in my tent at about 23,000 feet, my makeshift shelter tethered to some pickets hammered into the bulletproof ice. These were the only things holding me to the side of
the mountain. Below stretched an expansive, forty-five-degree-
steep glacier that fell for nearly a mile. But now something was
wrong. Incredibly wrong. I couldn't even think without getting
dizzy. My brain was swelling and I was suffering from extreme
anxiety and vertigo.

I knew I was dying . . . again.

✦

I grew up in a small, Midwest town called Willard, Ohio. It was just me, Mom, Dad, and my brother, Seth. Here, pretty much everyone knew your business. Most of the time that was fine, unless you were out doing something you probably shouldn't have been doing, like TP-ing the track coach's house. Of course then one of the neighbors would see you and your dad would get a call from someone who recognized you. Busted, again. Yeah, it seemed like I couldn't get away with anything. But that didn't stop me. It just forced me to be a little more, let's say... *resourceful* in order not to get caught.

As a kid I was very active in sports, and my family was always incredibly supportive. Whether I was playing YMCA soccer, swimming for the local league, playing football, or running track and cross country (heck, I even pole-vaulted, for crying out loud), Mom, Dad, and my brother were always there—they were my biggest fans.

I can still remember the brown, wooden house nestled off Hillcrest Drive, and the basketball hoop in the driveway where my dad and I would regularly challenge each other with a game of "H-O-R-S-E." I also used to love playing tennis against the garage and hear the ball slam off of the wooden door as it bounced back to me. Of course it usually didn't take long for Mom to come out and yell at me to go do something else—anything else as long as it was *somewhere* else.

When I wasn't playing sports, you could always find me out on some type of adventure. I had a huge cornfield in my backyard that alternated from feed corn to soy beans, depending upon the year. I always saw that field as my own little Imagination Land, just calling me to come out and explore. I'd build elaborate forts by bending the stalks over each other and then invite the other kids in the neighborhood come play with me. It was awesome!

Then—it must've been right around when I was eleven years old—I wanted to do something bigger, something better. I'm speaking, of course, about my impregnable underground fortress—the hole.

On the side of our house my dad had built a little shed that housed all of our tools. I had my pick of weed whackers, shovels, crow bars, and all sorts of other things a kid could kill himself with. It was awesome! One day, after months of planning and sketching, I was determined to get out there and build my underground fort - complete with concrete reinforcements and a "snorkel" where I could breathe while under the earth. What does one need in order to get underground? A shovel, of course! So I strolled out to the shed, flipped open the little slide lock, and grabbed the biggest shovel I could find. Hoisting it over my right shoulder, I headed out to the little sliver of land between my backyard and the cornfield. There I picked out the perfect spot, kicked my foot onto the top of the shovel head, and started digging. I pitched out my first load of dirt, dumping it far enough away from where my hole was going to be, and then went back in for more.

Shovelful after shovelful of dirt kept coming out of the hole and onto that pile. The hole kept getting deeper, and that pile of dirt kept getting bigger. I was making amazing progress. As I wiped the sweat from my forehead, I was sure that I was digging my way all the way down to China!

That is, until . . . *THWACK*! I hit something. And I hit it hard. At first, I tried chipping away at whatever was in the hole, but no matter how hard I kicked that shovel, I couldn't make a dent in this big, black, curved, tube-like thing. So I decided to just dig around it. The thing is, this big thing was right in the middle of the hole—my hole! Obviously, something had to be done.

I learned enough from watching my dad and listening to him while he was doing work around the yard that there were different types of shovels for different types of jobs. The one I had was for moving massive amounts of dirt, which was essentially what I was doing. But now I needed something thinner, something with a sharper blade to cut through this thing. The spade! Of course! So, dropping the load-hauling shovel, I ran back to the shed to grab the spade so I could get rid of that annoying thing that was taking up space where my hole should be.

Spade in hand, I proudly marched back to the future site of The Best Fort in the World. Once back at the hole, I was determined to remove the obstruction—whatever it was—even if it killed me. Hoisting the shovel up over my head, the thin, sharp blade pointing down at The Big Black Thing, a bead of sweat rolling down the tip of my nose, I thrust down on it with everything I had, smacking the immovable object with so much force that my hands slid down the shovel handle and I fell to my knees.

By this time I was a sweaty mess, covered in dirt from head to toe, and beyond frustrated—pissed, even—at whatever this thing was. All I knew was that this thing was in my hole and I wanted it out! Prying the spade underneath the object, I balanced on the end of the shovel and jumped, but still nothing happened. By this point I was livid. I started thinking about what else was in the shed that could possibly help me with this task, so I walked back and considered my options. Crow bar? Uh, uh. Shovel? Nope. Already tried two of those with no luck. What about the weed whacker? Nah. Besides, the orange extension cord wouldn't be long enough to make it out there anyways. Hedge trimmer? Same issue. A rusty saw? Possibly, but I didn't think I could get it down into the hole far enough to make any progress. Besides, with each stroke I'd probably just hit more dirt anyhow. My eyes darted back and forth. Which tool would be the right one for the job?

That's when I saw it—a red handle with a shiny and very sharp silver head. My dad's ax! Perfect! That thing would have no problem getting through that thing in the hole! So, as with the shovels, I swung the ax over my right shoulder and swaggered out again into the field to destroy this thing, this . . . whatever it was that was standing in the way of me building the world's most awesome subterranean fort.

What I didn't know was that every time I walked out from the side of the house with something swung over my shoulder, my dad, who was inside watching a football game, was casually watching me make the multiple trips from the shed to the field and back again. When he saw his son walking by with an incredibly sharp ax, which was about the same length as I was tall, my dad figured he should probably get involved.

Walking just far enough behind me so I didn't know he was there, Dad followed me out to where my genius idea was about to unfold. Then, right as I lifted the ax over my head and was getting ready to slam down on this annoying, black-plastic tube, I heard a voice from behind me say, "Boy, what do you think you're doing?"

I spun around and saw Dad standing behind me. I looked up at him, down at the hole, back at him, then back at the hole thinking it was a trick question. As I looked back at him one more time, I said "Um...I'm digging a hole?" Duh.

I don't think my dad was amused. "I can see that, dummy. But what do you think you're doing with that ax?"

I looked down at the sharp tool in my hand. "Oh . . . *thaaat*," I said. Of course there was no point in trying to hide it and pretend like he didn't see it, so I just told him the truth.

"Well, there's something in my hole, and I want it out."

"What is it you're trying to get out of *your* hole?" my dad said, as he approached the massive cavity in the cornfield, a.k.a., the Willard Grand Canyon. Standing at the rim of the crater, he just shook his head and let out a huge sigh.

"Seriously? You want to chop into that thing?"

"Well, yeah, dad. That's the only way to keep digging and finish my fort."

You see, all I knew at this point was A) I had a goal: dig a hole; B) I wanted to achieve that goal; and C) the only way to achieve my goal, i.e., dig a hole, was to get that thing, whatever it was, out of the way. That was my only focus.

Dad just glared at me. "Come up here," he said, "and let me show you something."

When I got up to the edge of the hole, my dad pointed down at the black plastic tube and started moving his arm up the length of the tube in the direction where it was coming from.

"Follow my fingers and look down that way. What do you see?"

Following his hand in the direction where the tube was coming from, I could see that it led all the way down the edge of the field into the little section of land that separated not just our house, but other homes and other properties.

"Yeah?" I said, not really sure what he was getting at.

"Keep going. What do you see?"

Then, continuing down the sight line, I could see a building half a mile or so away.

"That's the power plant. Yea? So?" I said, followed by a very long pause, while my brain put two and two together. "Oh my gosh! THE POWER PLANT!"

As it turns out, genius me was attempting to hack through the town's main electrical power line with a metal hatchet. Brilliant.

Dad just rolled his eyes. "Fill the hole back up, put the tools away, and meet me inside."

Thank goodness he came out when he did, or else I'd have been zapped into one crispy little critter.

Like I said, I was always getting into things, always looking for adventure. Little did I know one day it would lead me to the top of the world.

After my near-shocking encounter with The Big Black Thing, my run-of-the-mill Midwest upbringing rambled on. While my parents continued to do whatever it is that parents do, my brother and I went to countless swim meets and dodged trouble whenever we could, all the while trying to improve ourselves. Like Mom and Dad always said: "You don't have to be *THE* best—just be *YOUR* best." That struck a chord with me, and ever since, I've constantly compared myself to where I was yesterday, last week, last month, or last year, and then worked hard at improving myself, one step at a time.

It was a great childhood to be honest, and for the most part, everything was smooth sailing in our family. That is, until that one day, when everything in my life came to a screeching halt.

I remember it as clear as yesterday. It was after lunch and my friends and I were playing basketball in the multipurpose room before heading back to class. I went in for a lay-up, and when I came down to the wooden floor, my knee buckled and popped. Instantly everyone in the gym knew something was wrong, especially me. I felt the pain shoot up my leg, dart up my spine, and scream inside my brain. It was excruciating. Hobbling over to the makeshift stage in the Junior High gym, I sat down until the bell rang and then limped up to my eighth-grade science class. As I sat at my desk, all I wanted was for the day to be over and done with so I could go home and ice my knee. When the final bell rang, I made a beeline for home, not even bothering to stop by my locker to get my stuff.

When I finally got home, Mom was home waiting for me. Like all mom's, she immediately knew something was wrong. It could have been the agonized, worried look on my face that gave it away, or she could see that my knee had swollen to the size of a grapefruit. Something wasn't right. We immediately went to the local doctor, but he said he couldn't do anything because the swelling was already so advanced. So they contacted a specialist in Mansfield, about thirty minutes south. They were just closing up shop when we arrived but stayed open for one last x-ray. There was so much swelling, though, that they couldn't see what was going on inside the joint or around the area. So they wrapped my leg in an immobilizer to keep my knee from bending, gave me some crutches to hobble around on, and sent me on my way.

Crutches—sweet! I thought. This'll get the attention of ALL the chicks at school!

Sleeping that night was difficult to say the least, not because I couldn't roll around in bed, or because I couldn't sleep on my side in that oh-so-comforting fetal position, but because I couldn't wait to get to school and show off my new crutches!

The next day at school, the crutches worked better than I expected. Some of the cute girls actually carried my books from class to class. I wished the day would never end. But eventually the happiness and attention wore off, and I had to go home where my family would encourage me to try to do things for myself. Who does that, anyhow? What type of parents encourage their broken kid to do things on his own? Parents who want the best for their kid, that's who. Don't get me wrong, if it was something serious, they would have bent over backwards for me. But a bum leg? Nah. Rub some dirt in it and get on with things. That's just how they were. To be honest, I think it made me a stronger person in the long run.

The next morning, I somehow slept through my alarm clock, and Mom came to wake me up for school. She immediately called Dad into the room, and I'll never forget the look on their faces, as they stood there staring at me. Their eyes were the size of dinner plates, when Mom matter-of-factly said, "We better get him to the hospital."

Wait . . . what? Did I just hear that correctly? I'm going where? This might have been one of the few moments in my young life that I actually wanted to go to school. The hospital? Really? It was just a bum leg. Was this really necessary?

Luckily the hospital was only about a block and a half away from my house, so it didn't take long to get there. But when we pulled up and I could see the lighted "EMERGENCY" sign, I knew my situation was a lot more serious than just a bum knee. Once inside, the nurse rushed me to a small, square room with baby-blue walls where they shoved a needle in my arm and started drawing blood. Next, I was taken to another room for more x-rays, but this time of my chest. I can still hear the tech saying, "Okay, take a deep breath and hold," and then . . . zap! After that they put me in a wheelchair and took me upstairs to a room where I was to spend the next week. At first all the attention had been great, but this was going a little too far. I wanted to go home.

Apparently, there was something else the matter with me besides my knee, because the next thing I know they're treating me for pneumonia. But after a few days of sucking in fumes from a vaporizer, I wasn't showing any improvement. That's when Dr. Rosso came by to visit again and called Mom and Dad out to the hallway. As I watched them walk out of the room, I had no idea what was going on. It wasn't until later in life that they shared what had happened out there.

Once they were out in the hallway, my Dad began firing out questions. "What's going on? That's my first-born son in there. We haven't slept for a week, he's not getting any better, and . . ."

But Dr. Rosso just looked back at my parents with a vacant stare.

Like always, my mom knew. "Something's not right, is it?"

"Scott . . . Teri," the doctor began, "I'm not going to beat around the bush here. We really don't have much time. Do either of you know any oncologists?"

And there it was. The "O" word. It could only mean one thing: cancer. Their thirteen-year-old son had cancer.

Hearing that you have cancer is terrifying. Being diagnosed at thirteen with advanced Stage IV Hodgkin's Disease and told that you only have ninety days to live is an absolute nightmare. My parents thought me becoming a teenager was hard to accept, but this…this was inconceivable. I can't even imagine how they felt when the doctors gave them the news.

Having just three months to live puts everything into perspective. While my friends were all off worrying about the coolest shoes, the latest hairstyles, and being popular, I was lying in a hospital bed in Columbus, Ohio, fighting for my life. I would stare at the television, wondering what was going to show up in my compartmentalized, divided food tray that night. Did I even care? Not really. I just wanted to get out of there. I wanted my life back. Meanwhile, all that kept running through my brain was, *Why me?*

Because you did something to deserve this, replied a voice inside my head.

Shut up! I'd think. *You don't know what you're talking about.*

Yes, I do. You must have done something wrong to get put in this hospital and taken away from all of your friends.

Why me? Why me? Why me?

What is it, Sean? What did you do?

Shut up! Just SHUT UP!!!

The voices were driving me crazy. I had to do something about it.

Okay, I thought. *I'm in here. Something caused me to be in here, and I want to get out. I may never know 'Why me?', but in this instance, the fact is it IS me, and there's nothing I can do about it. Except fight! I want to be normal again! I have no idea what's in store for me, but like everything I've ever been taught, I'm going to do my best to overcome this crappy situation. Some things may be out of my control, but I'm going to do my best to control what I can... my thoughts!*

I had heard of the mind-body connection before, and how what the mind envisioned, the body could manifest. Then again, I didn't really know much about it. I had read a tiny bit on visualization, but still I didn't fully understand what it meant. I just knew it was something that could possibly help me in this situation. I had used my mind to help me with sports in the past—could it work here as well? I had always focused on being successful in the pool, and in the summer swim league I was undefeated. Obviously, I had done something right!

So I decided to keep my mind sharp and stay focused on the end result: my life being back to normal again.

I looked up at the bags of chemotherapy drugs and could feel the cool fluid rushing through my veins. How could something coming from a plastic bag with a radioactive symbol on it save my life (and without making my skin glow)? I began talking to myself again about what my options were at this point. It came down to two choices: either fight for my life or give up and die.

The answer was obvious.

Lying in the hospital bed after the first treatment, I thought to myself, *Hey, that wasn't so bad after all. All those horror stories of being nauseous, vomiting, and losing your hair...maybe they weren't true after all.* It was going to be just fine, I told myself as I adjusted the bed to the sleep position and drifted off into dreamland with a smile on my face.

I woke up violently ill. My stomach was burning and churning. The instant I opened my eyes, my salivary glands started watering and drool dripped from the corners of my mouth. That's when I felt the first wave of nausea overtake my body. Flinging the bed sheets off my sweating body, I knew I wasn't going to make it to the toilet. I had no control over what was happening. My stomach started retching until vomit spewed from my mouth, completely covering my lower body, and there wasn't a thing I could do. It was as if some demon was inside my stomach fighting to free itself.

Mom and Dad had been sleeping in the room with me, and they both were awakened by the vile sounds emitting from their son. Mom immediately called the nurses while Dad frantically searched for a trash can to put in front of my face.

This was only the beginning. It was the first true challenge of my life. For the next year, my body was a toxic, radioactive chemical dump of chemotherapy. I knew it was for the best, so I did what I could to keep a positive mindset. But behind those thoughts lurked the evil doubt of cancer.

The morning after my fourth treatment, I woke up and could feel that all-too-familiar morning pressure on my bladder. I swung my swollen feet to the edge of the bed and started to rock myself out, when, out of the corner of my eye, something caught my attention. My pillow looked like a dog with a severe shedding problem had slept on it. Obviously, I knew that wasn't the case. I couldn't believe my eyes. This was one of the worst things that could possibly happen. It was what I'd dreaded and feared the most. That was my hair! From my head!

My hands trembled as I gently brushed away the hairs that only hours before had been attached to my head. I sobbed uncontrollably. In a panic I scooped up the hair and ran to the bathroom to see where it had all come from. Maybe it was only a small patch. Maybe nobody would notice. Maybe I could cover it up. Then again, maybe not. Staring into the mirror, I didn't even recognize the person looking back at me. I used to be the embodiment of fitness and health. Now the dark bags under my eyes made me look like I hadn't slept in months, and my once athletic swimmer's body was approaching the limits of obesity. I choked back the tears, telling myself, "I'm tough. I can handle this."

I turned on the shower, understanding what was coming next was going to be difficult, but it was something I had to do. Leaning forward, I could feel the warm water against my scalp. I worked the shampoo up into a lather and prepared myself for what I knew was going to be a traumatic experience. Feeling my fingers work their way through the remaining hair on my scalp, my hands began to tremble. Slowly, I pulled my hands off my head and into view, and I was horrified to see they were absolutely covered in hair. I couldn't breathe. I collapsed onto the shower floor, pulling chunks of hair out of the drain so the water could flow out. I just sat there crying, in utter shock. Everything I ever wanted from life was now so far out of reach. How was I ever going to get through this? Would I even survive the day?

I don't know how long I was in there, but it must have been quite a while, because when I started coming back to reality, I was shivering uncontrollably. The water, no longer warm, was like flowing ice. Every single hair on my teenage head had fallen out—eyebrows, eyelashes...everything.

I was a bona fide freak.

It took a long time, but eventually I decided that, no matter what I looked like, I would always remain true to myself and who I was raised to be. Cancer could take my hair, it could even ruin my body, but it would never take my mind, my sense of humor, or my determination to make it through this and get my life back. I had cancer. There was nothing I could do about it but deal with it and focus on getting back to being normal again. Having these constant positive thoughts and affirmations flowing through my mind overwhelmed the negative thoughts and pushed them from my brain.

I continued to visualize and focus on the end—getting healthy and normal again. Every night I would picture myself swimming again, coming out of the water a champion. Every time I had a treatment and the cool toxic chemicals were pumped into my veins, I would visualize the chemo going into my body where a battle of epic proportions was taking place.

Each little molecule of fluid was a micro-spaceship. I became the drop of chemo that fell out of the bag and into the clear plastic tube connected to my veins. Dropping out of the bag and falling into the liquid reservoir, I'd patiently await my turn to be sucked into the launching platform of the IV tube. Meanwhile, I'd quickly perform my pre-flight check to make sure all the guns were armed with only the best chemo available. Looking out past the clear, plastic IV tube into the hospital room, I could see my own body lying on the transformer bed… the nurse leaving the room . . . my mom sitting by my side . . . the TV showing some old rerun.

Then, all of a sudden, the bright hospital room would disappear as I was violently sucked into the bloodstream among the red and white blood cells and jolted into the body. Navigating my ship, I'd look at the dashboard GPS system to see the location of my target—the foreign substance I was created to destroy. Navigating my ship through the veins, I could hear the beating of the heart getting louder and louder as my team of expert fighters and other captains prepared to get hurtled to all corners of the body to defeat the enemy.

Getting closer to the command center, I would see the valve of the heart opening and closing with each beat. Feeling the ebb and flow of the life-support system of blood, I'd quickly get sucked into the heart where the noise was deafening. Lub-dub! Lub-dub! Lub-dub! Watching the rest of the crew and ships get shot out of the heart, I would prepare for my mission. Time would slow down and I'd be even more aware of every detail until, finally, I'd get thrust out of the heart as my hunt for the aliens began.

My ship would dart through the veins of the body—a left turn here, a right there. Where the veins split, I'd look at my console and follow the blips leading me to the cancer cells I was responsible for killing. I'd continue to fly through the body until I found the cluster I was to destroy, and then . . . BOOM! A surprise attack! They'd never see me coming!

"Engage the missiles! Fire the cannons! Shoot the lasers! Let's give these morons everything we have until they're dead!" And with that, my entire ship would erupt in one giant explosion of firepower, sending the chemo directly into the heart of the beast!

Every time I received a treatment, I'd focus my mind and visualize this internal battle happening inside of my body, and I would picture the chemotherapy "ships" destroying the evil cancer "aliens." Chemo Space Invaders, if you will. I pictured every single little detail in order to make it as real as I could, and involved as many senses as possible, while at the same time keeping my mind focused on one image: me swimming back and forth at the league meet—and coming out a champion.

Nearly a year went by as I battled the cancer. These were some of the hardest days of my life. I gained about seventy pounds and lost every strand of hair on my body. I lost my myself. In a way, I lost my life for a while. Everything was so different. I was different. I felt powerless and, at times, hopeless. Why couldn't this all be over? Why did I have to go through this? Why couldn't I just be a normal, healthy kid? Why? Lying there in my bed, the seconds blurred into minutes, the days into weeks. On the good days (i.e., when I wasn't taking any medicine), the time would fly by. But, then, when I was injected with more medicine, time would slow to a crawl.

Yet, despite it all, I never lost focus on my goal: winning the 50m breaststroke championship. Having goals kept my mind focused on the future. Sure, I loved living in the present, but at that moment the present was just too horrible. It was nothing but blood tests and chemo and prednisone . . . and only God knows what else. In order to survive, in order to get through the terrible present, I had to force myself to focus on something, anything, in the future.

In the rare times I felt well enough to exercise, I would push by body beyond what I thought it could handle. I wasn't about to waste the few good days being lazy and doing nothing. I'd save the relaxing for when I was receiving the treatments and pretending to be Interplanetary Body Captain Spaceman Spiff—my cancer-fighting alter-ego. I looked forward to the good days, and I wasn't about to waste them sitting around feeling sorry for myself.

I did what I could when I could. Sometimes I'd go out to run around the neighborhood or even tag along with the cross-country team during their practice. I didn't want to be excluded from things simply because I was different. I thought having another smaller goal could help me get to that swimming championship, so I decided to train for a local 5k run. The way I saw it, it would help keep my body in decent cardiovascular shape during my treatments, and it would also get the endorphins going. It was just a small goal, but it kept me focused on something other than my current situation.

Believe it or not, just one week after a chemo treatment I achieved my goal and finished that 5k! Did I win? Not even close. In fact, I finished dead last. But I had focused my mind on a goal, accomplished that goal, and had a heck of a lot of fun doing it. The only thing that mattered was that I had accomplished something that helped build my confidence for future challenges and adventures. Like the swimming championship.

I spent a year doing smaller events like running the 5k, participating in local YMCA soccer matches, and trying to win the neighborhood hide-and-seek competitions. These little things boosted my confidence and got me out of the house (when I wasn't throwing up, that is). They also taught me to have fun, and through all these little victories, I learned that my body could handle whatever I put it through because my mind was in charge.

I could've just given up and felt sorry for myself. I could have let the cancer and the chemo and everything else beat me down and control my emotions. But instead I stayed active and kept my mind focused on the end result, which was so vivid and real in my mind. I knew I would get there. I knew I would make my dream a reality.

Finally, a year after being diagnosed with cancer, Dr. Davis told my family I was in remission, and I only had a few more chemo treatments left, just to make sure all the cancer cells were destroyed. I can't tell you how happy I was to hear that. I dreaded the treatments. They made me wretch and vomit uncontrollably for days on end, and because of a muscular allergic reaction to one of the anti-nausea medications, at one point my eyeballs actually rolled back into my head and left me temporarily blind. On top of that, I was seventy pounds overweight, I had no hair on any part of my body, and I had blisters inside my mouth and sores chapping my skin. There was even one time when I had a temperature of 108, and had an out-of-body experience where I floated above my body with the Grim Reaper and saw my own corpse lying on the bed below.

Any these things could have made me quit. But they didn't. I was too focused on one simple thing: getting my life back to normal. Was it worth it? Without a doubt. Was it easy? Not. One. Bit.

Sliding into the water for the first time after they removed my Hickman Catheter (a permanent IV sticking out of my chest that was surgically implanted so I wouldn't have to get a needle stuck in me every time I went in for a treatment), I knew I had a long road ahead of me if I ever wanted to win another race. But I was so excited to be back at home in the water. I couldn't wait to start zipping back and forth in the pool and feel like my old self again. This was it. I had made it back!

The first couple strokes felt great—slow, but great. The feeling didn't last though. After swimming down and back the length of the pool just one time, I was out of breath and exhausted. One time! My heart felt like it was pounding out of my chest. My arms, well...my arms felt like they had fallen off and sunk to the bottom of the pool. I was so frustrated. I actually had to use the ladder to get out of the water—I wasn't strong enough to pull myself out. Throwing my goggles across the deck, I grabbed my towel and ran into the bathroom. It was hopeless. How was I ever going to get back to where I once was? How could I even imagine winning anything ever again?

I flopped onto the bench in the locker room, completely deflated. My towel over me, my head in my hands, I just stared down at my feet and cried. *This is impossible,* I thought. *There's no way I'll ever get back to where I want to be.*

Just then I felt a hand on my back and heard a familiar voice. "You can do this." I turned to see my younger brother, Seth, standing behind me. He had followed me into the locker room knowing I was incredibly frustrated.

Seth had done so many things for me throughout the previous year, but I had no clue until later in life. For example, once he overheard a group of kids talking about how fat and ugly I was, and how I shouldn't be allowed out of the house. Seth went up to them and told them why I looked like I did, and how they shouldn't make fun of someone who's fighting for their life. Maybe one day *they'd* be fighting cancer, he told them. How would *they* like it if people made fun of *them*?

Best brother ever.

And now here he was, standing behind me, encouraging me to get up and try again.

So that's just what I did.

I never compared myself with others. I just wanted to do better than I did the day before, than the week before. I just took it one day, one hour, one minute at a time.

Day after day I'd push myself a little further, a little harder. My parents would drive me to the YMCA pool over in Shelby so I could practice without being ridiculed. This continued until I felt like I was ready to be seen by my friends and teammates in my oh-so-flattering Speedo.

Finally it was time for the summer swim league championship. I had been working on my visualization every night for months, picturing myself getting out of the water in first place. I had put in the time. I had pushed my body to the limit, and my mental state could not have been any better. This was it. And I was ready.

The day of the big race, my race—the 50m breaststroke—my family was in the stands and ready to cheer me on. This hadn't just been my battle. It had been incredibly hard on them, too. Now they were here to support me and celebrate how far I had come—how far we all had come.

I stood on the deck getting my mind ready as I went through my warmup routine, flapping my arms back and forth, in circles forward together, then backward together, and then the cocky one arm forward, one arm backward. I looked up at the starting block where the race was about to begin. Placing my goggles over my eyes, I focused on the wall below, where I pictured myself finishing first countless times. Not just by a fraction of a second, but by body lengths ahead of the competition.

TWEET! TWEET! The official's whistle pierced through the air signaling that it was time for my heat. The starter's voice echoed throughout the pool. "Swimmers . . . step up!"

My heart was pounding. *Here we go. This is it. All that pain. All that hard work. Now it pays off.* Breathing deeply, I stepped up onto the starting block, tall and confident. My eyes were drawn to the other end of the pool where I saw my teammates waiting to cheer me on.

"Take your mark!"

I placed my left foot at the end of the starting block, my toes curled around the edge. My right foot stayed back for the staggered, quicker start I had practiced thousands of times before. My hands reached to the front, outside of the blocks, and curled under the metal where I could feel the sandpaper-like traction from the top folded underneath. I took one more deep breath, and then...

"BANG!"

The gun went off and the crowd erupted as I launched myself out into the air, arms forward, piercing the surface of the water like a knife. The outside world disappeared. Total silence—the only sound was my own voice inside my head encouraging me, driving me forward.

I felt myself slowing down and pulled my arms under my body to push myself forward and glide until I started slowing again. Bringing my arms under my chest, my legs up to my body, I kicked and finished my pullout. With a strong pull my body thrust forward as my head popped above water, and my own inner voice was suddenly joined by those of the frenzied onlookers. The noise was deafening. I took in a breath before my head went underwater again. Another breath as my head came above water. The cheers grew louder. Bubbles formed around my ears. The voice in my head kept pushing me on. *Harder! Faster!* Adrenaline surged through my veins as I got closer and closer to the turn.

Touching the wall to turn back for the last lap, my hand skimmed by my ear, my feet swooped up to the wall, and my head flew back to help create momentum. All my teammates were there cheering for me, shouting my name. They were all a blur except for one who caught my eye.

"YOU CAN DO THIS!" It was Seth. He was right there, front and center, cheering me on. It gave me an extra boost of energy as I pushed off the wall for the sprint to the finish.

Stroke after stroke, amidst the deafening sound of cheers and the utter silence underwater, I made my way closer and closer to the wall. Lactic acid was building inside my muscles as my arms pushed the water away and my legs thrust me forward. The burn grew more and more intense with every stroke. My lungs screamed for air each time my head broke the water.

Keep going! You got this! Harder! HARDER!

Then, with one final stroke, I lunged out and touched the wall. I immediately ripped off my goggles and looked to my left, looked to my right—no one. I turned to see the second-place finisher coming in. He was body lengths behind me! It was exactly how I had pictured it in my mind hundreds of times before. And now it had all come true! All my hard work. All the struggling through pain and self-doubt. All those little things that could have stopped me but didn't because I was so focused on my goal, on the end result. It had finally paid off, and now here I was, champion of the 50m breaststroke!

The timer, who by the way just happened to be my dad, reached out and pulled me out of the water to give me the biggest hug ever. "I'm so proud of you!" he said, as the rest of the team came to congratulate me. I also wanted to congratulate the other swimmers. I wanted to thank them for encouraging me and for pushing me to be my best. I was back! And on top of that, I was a force to be reckoned with!

Note: I later found out that I had broken the league record. Last I heard, it's still standing today.

Chapter 2

Entering high school was fairly easy for me because we lived in a small town and everyone already knew my history and that I had overcome cancer in the eighth grade. While the low kids on the totem pole, so to speak, were getting wedgies and having their books knocked out of their arms, I was left alone. Maybe they just figured I had been through enough already. Maybe they felt sorry for me. Whatever the reason, I was happy for it, and "initiation" into the cross-country team family was nothing. I was welcomed with open arms.

By this point, all I cared about was being normal. When I was sick, seventy pounds overweight, and bald from head to toe, I had stuck out like a sore thumb. My wig gave me some level of comfort and made me feel somewhat normal again, but it just wasn't me. I wasn't me. While my friends had been out chasing girls, collecting baseball cards, and just generally having a great time, my life had been on pause for an entire year as I fought to survive.

That said, while they were busy worrying about who had the coolest hairstyle, the nicest shoes, or who was the most popular, I was learning to focus on what truly was important: being myself and doing the best I could, every single day of my life. It was during those dark times when I was knocking on Death's Door that I learned to enjoy every day as though it was my last, because, no matter what I do, no matter what any of us do, one day it will be. Shouldn't we take advantage of all the opportunities we have right now? I certainly thought so.

Being "normal" took on a different meaning for me. I couldn't really relate to others with their obsession over material things. Why did people want to be like everyone else instead of who they were themselves? Was it jealousy? Insecurity? Why do people idolize celebrities simply because they're famous? Did they really think money could buy them happiness? I couldn't figure any of it out. All I knew was I had just spent a year in and out of the hospital fighting for my life, and it put everything into perspective.

After everything I had gone through, I decided as a freshman in high school that I was going to focus what was really important. I was going to focus on being me.

I loved being back to normal. Back to being myself again. Strolling around the halls of Willard High, without a care in the world, my future looked bright. (Incredible, considering that it wasn't that long ago I had been given just a few months to live.) My monthly check-ups were all coming back negative, the cancer was in remission, and I was on cloud nine. Everything was wonderful.

Then one day, twenty months after being declared healthy again, I went to the hospital for my routine check-up, and I just knew something wasn't right. Over the years, I had become pretty in-tune with my body and what my physiology was telling me. It wasn't too difficult, to be honest. All I had to do was listen to it and not freak out over every little thing that went wrong. You can't be emotional and logical at the same time, so I learned how to take deep breaths when I felt overcome with emotion and, therefore, fend off any impending doom and anxiety about the cancer returning.

But this time was different. My body was telling me something just wasn't right, specifically inside my chest on the right side.

As was the norm, I sat down at the all-too-familiar chair with the rest for my elbow. The nurse scooted over on her four-wheeled stool with alcohol pad, giant rubber band, and needle in hand. After cleaning the skin with the alcohol, she wrapped the giant rubber band around my upper arm to get my veins to bulge out so she could decide which one to puncture this time. As she pushed the needle through my flesh and into the same veins in which I had flown my micro-spaceship during chemotherapy (Interplanetary Body Captain Spaceman Spiff, remember?), I could see the dark red blood shoot out into the vial. I wondered if they'd find any remnants of the internal battle I'd waged against the alien invaders.

The nurse removed the needle, applied a Band-Aid, and told me to keep on trucking to the next station. The folks at x-ray were used to scanning older people with cancer, so whenever I arrived in the basement of the hospital for my monthly photo shoot, they were always happy to see a young, smiling face.

Shirt off. Check! Shoulders forward. Check! Deep breath. Don't move. Say cheese! And . . . *zap!*—my bones were recorded.

Back in the doctor's office, my parents and I patiently waited for the "wet reading" of the blood work and for Dr. Davis to get the x-rays sent to his office. This was the fastest way to analyze the results, and it enabled them to quickly take care of whatever nastiness might be lurking inside my body.

"Hmmm…that's interesting," Dr. Davis said after reviewing my x-ray in the office light. Then, tapping the bones of my chest with his pen, he leaned his head to the left. "We're going to have to see what that is in order to get a better look at it."

I wasn't sure what the private conversation between my parents and my oncologist was all about, but the next thing I know I was being prepped for a needle biopsy in another area of the hospital. Turns out that in my x-ray, Dr. Davis had noticed a mass on my right lung, right between my ribs and my lungs. They needed to determine if it was benign (non-cancerous) or—heaven forbid, not again!—malignant. Either way, it had to be removed. I had a tumor in my chest, and it was affecting my breathing. For the past week, whenever I breathed in deeply, it felt like I was being stabbed in the chest with a knife. One night I even cried myself to sleep because of the pain.

Now I was laying on a surgical table preparing myself to have a six-inch needle threaded through my ribs and into this mass on my chest wall. Trust me, all those sharp pokes from small numbing needles were nothing compared to what was about to be shoved past my ribs.

"Try and breathe very slowly," said someone to my right as I looked at the TV screen to my left, which showed the location of the tumor. I tried to stay calm and maintain slow breaths while the stainless-steel needle punctured my skin, slid past my ribs, and found its way into the fuzzy spot on the screen. I was fascinated by the process and what they were doing. Then again, this was my lung they were going into, and it was my body they were invading, so I closed my eyes, focused on my breathing, and tried to relax so that the experts could do their thing.

Eight long hours later, the results of the needle biopsy came back. It wasn't good. Not good at all.

My family and I were sitting in the room waiting for Dr. Davis to come in and talk to us about the biopsy and next steps. But then when he came in, he asked Mom and Dad to step outside into the hallway so he could speak to them in private. That wasn't going to happen. At this point I was nearly sixteen years old, and just like everyone else that age, I was nosey as nelly, especially when it came to adults talking about me. I needed to know what was going on. So summoning as much strength as I could, I leaned forward, grabbed my little buddy (i.e., my IV pole) and shuffled closer to the door so I could hear their conversation.

Mom didn't beat around the bush at all. "Is it cancer again?" she asked. Her voice trembled, and I could hear her choking back tears.

That's when the doc confirmed my family's worst fear. "I'm afraid it is, Teri."

Cancer had reared its ugly head . . . again.

I didn't care what the rest of the conversation was about. The word "cancer" was all I need to hear. I turned and made my way back to the hospital bed, where I buried my face in the pillow and began to cry. I had already gone through hell with the first cancer. I couldn't imagine going through it all over again. I just couldn't. My life was over. There was no way I could deal with those awful treatments again. I didn't want to lose my hair again. I didn't want to lose my friends again. I didn't want to lose my *life* again. No way was this happening. Not again. Why me? What did I do? Why was I being punished—again!?

What in the world, God? I guess once wasn't enough!? You had to give me cancer twice?!

To make matters worse, I was diagnosed with Askin's Sarcoma, a type of cancer that affects only three out of one million people and that has a survivability rate of roughly 6 percent. That means that if 100 people are diagnosed with this new type of cancer, ninety-four of them don't make it. The vast majority of them die. No one else in the entire world, in the history of cancer, had ever been diagnosed with both Hodgkin's Disease and Askin's Sarcoma. Not a single one. Lucky me. There was no precedent, no protocol to follow. I was about to become a medical guinea pig, pumped with a chemical cocktail that had little chance of ridding my body of this deadly disease.

That was, *if* I made it past the next two weeks. Fourteen days—that's all the time I was given to live.

Not long after the "C word" was uttered again, I was back on the gurney being ushered into surgery prep. Regardless of whether the tumor was benign or malignant, it still needed to be removed, and the quicker the better. I had been having my check-ups for the Hodgkin's Disease once a month for a year before cutting back to once every three months. When I was still showing "clean" signs, the doc wanted to make it once every six months, but my family and I agreed we wanted it to bump it up to every four months, just to be safe. Thank God we did. My previous chest x-ray from my check-up four months earlier had come back negative, meaning I had clean scans and my chest was clear. But now here I was with a painful tumor in my chest, and it needed to be removed.

If you've ever had surgery before, you know how the operating room is always freezing cold. It literally feels like you're being wheeled into a refrigerator. Nothing was different this time, so they stacked a bunch of warm blankets on top of me to keep me from shivering. Though, I'm not quite sure if I was shaking from the cold or from being nervous about what was about to happen.

I leaned forward to ask for the surgeon before they doped me up enough to knock me out. As the surgeon came to my side, I said, "Doc . . . I know chicks dig scars. So make this a good one, would ya?" Nothing like a little humor to calm the nerves. "Oh, and could you please do me a favor?"

"Sure," he said. "What's that?"

"Please don't forget to put everything back in, okay?"

"Don't worry, Sean," he replied with a smile. "We'll take good care of you. And I'll do my best to only take out the bad stuff. We'll leave all the good stuff in there."

Last thing I remember is falling asleep with a smile on my face as the anesthesia washed over my body and put me into a state of unconsciousness.

Chapter 3

My eyes slowly opened as I looked around the small, curtain-partitioned room. Nothing looked familiar. I was alone, and I had no idea where I was. I struggled to think clearly. The only thing I recognized was the distant beep, beep, beep of the machine that let me know my heart was still working. Gradually I drifted off to sleep again.

Somewhere far off, I could hear voices, people talking. I couldn't understand what they were saying, but I knew they were talking to me, asking me questions. The voices grew louder. I could hear chattering in the distance. Voices over speakers telling someone to go somewhere. More people seemed to be walking around near me. Something touched my arm. I could feel it lightly brushing the back of my hand. The noise slowly grew louder. The room became brighter. I opened my eyes to my mom holding my hand. Dad was standing right next to her. Thank goodness I wasn't alone. It was so incredibly comforting to have them there. Seth was just to my left, staring at me, wondering how his big brother was doing after such a grueling surgery to remove a golf-ball-sized tumor.

My throat and mouth were parched thanks to the tube they shoved down my throat while I was in surgery. Of course, I'd been there, done that before, so it was a familiar feeling. But this time around it was so much worse. I was horribly dry and could barely even speak.

In the distance, past the foot of my bed, I could see a blurry figure walking toward me with a smile on her face. She had a gentle calmness about her, and as she approached me she asked if there was anything she could get or do for me. My brain still wasn't fully functional, so I didn't quite grasp the fact that she was a nurse and there to help me. I just shook my head up and down, attempting to communicate non-verbally with this strange being.

"Okay," she said. "What would you like, Sean?"

Sean? Well, at least she knew my name. That was a good thing, right? I tried to put together a simple three-letter word—ice—to soothe my burning, dry throat. But all I could manage was, "Uff." *Uff? What the [explicative] is that? Think, you moron! Tell her what you need!*

"Uff." *Seriously? What in the world is going on inside my brain?*

I could tell this woman was just as confused as me. Her head was cocked to the side like a dog's when it doesn't under-stand something. I'm sure she had no idea what "Uff" meant. Then again, neither did I.

As she started to turn and walk away, somehow, I managed to get something out that made a little more sense. "Frozen water."

A smile appeared on her face. "You mean, you want some *ice*?"

Again, I nodded, so glad that we had gotten past the communication barrier. She left the room and moments later was back with a Dixie cup full of chipped ice. I instantly tossed it into my mouth to let the cold meltwater soothe my burning throat.

It took a few days, but gradually I emerged from the haze and became more aware. It was clearly apparent that something was different about me. Something on my right side. Every breath, no matter how small, brought excruciating pain, and rightfully so, because I had a few broken ribs from the surgery. Under my right arm there was a pillow in the shape of a lung. This would become my security blanket during my recovery. Meanwhile I sucked in breaths from a corrugated tube that measured my lung capacity and strength. With each painful breath, I watched the accordion-like balloon rise up off its circular base before collapsing once again.

I had no idea what was ahead of me or how rough life was about to become. Since Askin's Sarcoma is such an aggressive, deadly form of cancer, the treatments this second time around would be much harder on my body. On top of that, no one had ever had these two cancers together before, so the doctors weren't really sure what to do. They just started tossing everything they had at me.

In the meantime I began to visualize a goal. Something to work toward as I went through the worst of the treatment and the recovery. I started off by focusing on one extremely important goal: to pee on my own. This may sound trivial to you, but it was a huge deal to me. Do you know how embarrassing it is to be a teenager and have to tell the nurses that you soiled the sheets—again? Heck, it was bad enough when I was going through my first cancer and lying in a constant puddle of puke. Now it was coming out of both ends. Something had to be done.

I began by figuring out the steps to success and then focusing on them one at a time. I knew I had to start with getting out of the hospital bed. After that I had to work my way over to the wheelchair so I could push myself to the bathroom. It wasn't easy, but after a couple days I was finally able to go to the bathroom on my own.

One step at time.

Once that initial goal was accomplished, I focused on bigger ones. Next, I built up my strength until I could wheel myself around the nurses' station. Then it was around the floor of the hospital wing. After that it was the entire hospital. They were just small steps, small successes, but they all added up to the ultimate goal: remission.

My chemotherapy cycles began right out of the gate. Askin's is a rapidly growing cancer, and the medical team didn't want to waste any time. I started with inpatient therapy, meaning I was in the hospital when receiving my treatments. Initially, they prescribed three months of treatments. I'd spend Monday to Friday in the hospital, and then I'd be released over the weekend to recover before starting the whole process over again on

Monday. So after a week-long cycle of treatment, they'd release me to let my body heal itself and increase my blood count before hitting me again with the same, horrible treatment. If my counts didn't come back high enough—which was entirely possible and happened often—the chemotherapy would kill me. But as long as my counts were high enough, I'd go back in to finish the other half of the cycle.

Because this treatment was so devastating on the body and the side effects are absolutely horrendous, the doctors didn't want me to remember any of it. So whenever I was in the hospital, I was placed into a medically-induced coma. I wouldn't remember throwing up constantly or soiling the sheets, which, I guess, was a good thing. But what also happened was that, essentially, I lost an entire year of my life. I don't remember being sixteen at all, except for one month, and it was in September when I was receiving my radiation treatments. It's as if that year of my life never existed.

After three months of torture with the chemotherapy, it was time for the radiation therapy. Monday through Friday, I would lie on my back and get gamma radiation shot through my right lung. Luckily the immediate side effects for that weren't nearly as harsh. The long-term effects, however, were a little more devastating, since it ended up destroying my right lung and making it incapable of transferring oxygen. In the end I was essentially left with just one lung.

Following the month-long radiation, I started back up on those wonderful chemotherapy cycles again—this time for more than ten months. It took over a year before I was declared in remission again. Meanwhile my friends were all out getting their driver's licenses, going on dates, and doing all the other things that normal teenagers do. It all seemed so unfair.

That said, my focus was so different than theirs. They were worried about being cool. I was just worried about staying alive. When you go through something like this, when you're given just fourteen days to live and forced to look at your own mortality, it changes you. This was changing me. The cancer, the treatments, the pain—it was all changing me. And I knew it. I didn't know how, exactly, but I knew that it was having an impact on my life and changing me in some fundamental type of way. How, exactly, only time would tell.

In the fall of 1993, five years after I had been diagnosed with cancer the first time and given just three months to live, I embarked on the next phase of my life: college.

Westminster College is a small, Presbyterian school in the even smaller town of New Wilmington, Pa., smack in the heart of Western Pennsylvania Amish territory. You wouldn't think it would be a wild place, but believe me (I hope Mom and Dad don't read this part), my time there was just one, big, four-and-a-half-year-long party! If you've ever seen the movie "Animal House," well . . . it was sorta like that. And I loved every minute of it.

Initially I was majoring in molecular biology, thinking I was going to splice genes and cure cancer, but as it turns out, it's hard to do well in classes like Organic Chemistry or Immunology when you hardly ever open a textbook, and you're living every day like a rock star.

Halfway through my junior year, I switched to psychology. I thought it would be fun and might give me some guidance on what to do with the rest of my life. (Spoiler alert: It didn't.) And since I had changed my major so late in the game, I had to stick around an extra semester for a class that was only offered in the fall. Luckily, it was only one day a week. Of course this only provided more time for my beer-pong practice and other Belushi-esque, party animal habits.

College came and went (too fast, of course), and I graduated with an incredibly impressive 2.8 GPA. As you can imagine, graduate schools were knocking down my door, tossing scholarship money my way in the hopes that I'd bring my amazing intellect and work ethic to their program. Actually, no, that's not how it happened at all. In fact, it was pretty much the opposite. However, thanks to my high GRE scores, which I was told were the highest the psychology department had ever seen (go figure), I did get accepted to a number of schools in the U.K. But none of them offered any financial support, and since I didn't have an extra 35,000 British Pounds in my back pocket, I ended up applying to some schools in the southern U.S. and got accepted to one in Florida.

Graduate school took me thousands of miles away from home and my comfort zone, but it also gave me an opportunity to reflect on my life. I was working on my doctorate (believe it or not) to become a psycho-oncologist—a psychologist for cancer patients—while at the same time holding down three jobs in order to afford all of my bills and tuition. During this time I started thinking about how in the world I ended up Florida and if my life had any meaning.

During my high school years when I was battling cancer, I didn't have time to think about the big picture. I was too busy just trying to survive and make it to the next day. Now, here I was in Florida, and I finally stopped to think about where I had come from and all I had been through.

Looking back on the footsteps of my long, difficult journey, I realized that every step I'd taken had been a decision that I had made on my own. I could've done nothing and just let the cancer eat me alive, but I didn't. Instead I made a conscious decision to fight and set certain goals for myself—no matter how small or seemingly inconsequential—and didn't stop until I achieved those goals.

Just about every single person on Earth has a say in what they do, where they go, and what goals they set for themselves. All my past choices, all the decisions I had ever made for myself, both good and bad, had brought me to where I was right now. And although we can't change our past and who we are, we have every opportunity to change our future. My past had already been written. The path that had brought me to where I was now could not be changed. But my future was mine to control. I had the power to decide how I wanted it to be, and with the right choices, I could have whatever life I wished to live. I could find happiness. I could find my purpose. I could become a doctor of psychology and work in a hospital helping people like me who had been touched by cancer.

The thing is, that's not what I wanted.

There were so many times during my battles with cancer when I felt hopeless, when I felt like I was dying. Countless nights I'd fall asleep not knowing if I was even going to wake up the next morning. You want to talk about being scared? Try closing your eyes and not knowing if you're ever going to wake up again.

In high school I was known as "Cancer Boy" and basically lost an entire year of my life when I was sixteen. In college, I tried to make up for all those years that had been taken from me. As a result, I turned into a wild and crazy party animal with lackluster grades and no direction in life.

Now I was in graduate school and finally thinking about my life and my future. This was incredibly difficult for me. For so much of my young life, my future—if I made it through the night—was simply the next day. This was the first time I had even considered my long-term future, and I realized that I didn't want to become a psychologist for cancer patients. I had my own "cancer baggage" to deal with. How could I help others when I still needed help myself?

I was at a crossroads in my life with no map to guide me. Should I just suck it up, continue with my doctorate, and then go on to be a psycho-oncologist? Should I continue surfing during the week and bartending on the weekends, forever questioning my own potential and ability? I didn't know which way to turn.

Then, one night while I was bartending at a nightclub in Jacksonville Beach, it all became so clear. An incredibly sexy and beautiful girl approached the bar to order a drink. "Sex on the Beach and your phone number, please."

As the bass thumped in the background, I flashed her a flirtatious smile and went off to make her drink. I slid the drink across the bar, and as she reached out to grab it, I grabbed her hand. Pulling her close to me, I leaned in and whispered into her ear, "Hang around later and let's get together."

The girl smiled back at me, and as she walked away, I knew I would see her again. She kept coming back for more drinks, and every time she did, we would flirt across the bar. Strutting out to the dance floor, she'd keep an eye on me while she moved her body in an oh-so-smooth and sexy way.

Finally, last call came and she sat down on the stool directly across from me. She told me her friends had left her and asked if I could take her home.

Oh, yeah! I thought, but trying to play cool on the outside I said, "Yea. I guess can do that."

Minutes later we were in my car on our way back to her place. We hadn't gotten very far, however, before she asked me to pull over because she was going to—yep, you guessed it—throw up. I yanked the wheel to the side of the road and slammed on the brakes just in time for her to projectile vomit all over the blacktop. How lovely.

"I'm so sorry," she said, as wave after wave of whatever was in her stomach kept coming up and out.

I had a bottle of water with me, so after she was finished being sick, I offered it to her and continued driving to her apartment.

What in the world am I doing? I thought to myself. *This isn't me. This never was me. I'm better than this.*

Following her mumbling directions, I managed to find her apartment complex. Fortunately, she had given me her apartment number before she passed out. After parking the car, I went around to the passenger side, pulled her out, and then carried her up three flights of stairs to the door marked "C3." I had no idea who or what was behind the door, or even if it was the right place, but I just kicked it until someone opened it. Some girl, who looked like death warmed over, stood in the doorway. Behind her a group of guys were sitting on the couch playing video games.

Still holding the lifeless lump of a human being in my arms, I walked straight past the girl and into the room. Not sure what to say, I just blurted out the first thing I could think of. "Does she belong to you guys?"

"Ha!" laughed some crackhead in the corner. "Again?"

I looked over at the coffee table and could see lines of white powder and needles next to blackened spoons. I had to get out of there—fast! Putting the drunken girl down in a lounge chair near the door, I made a quick exit and headed back to my car. I drove home in a daze, glad that I had done the right thing. Luckily, I hadn't been killed for doing it.

That night changed my life, and I knew it was time to get out of the club scene. Bartending just wasn't the right path for me, but, then again, neither was becoming a psychologist. I needed a new direction, a new path. And it looked like I was going to have to make my own way.

At this particular fork in the road, I could have gone left, or I could have gone right. I decided to go straight.

I did a lot of self-reflection over those next few weeks. I still wasn't sure what I wanted to do, but I knew I wanted to do something big. Something amazing. I needed to give people something I never had when I was sick: hope.

Seth had just graduated from college, and moved in with me to help me come up with an idea. I knew I wanted to change the lives of people touched by cancer. During my own personal battles with the disease, there were many times when I didn't have an ounce of hope. Now, as a survivor, I knew life was too precious and too short to take for granted. I wanted to share this with as many people as possible. The question was, how?

I needed a stage. A platform. But it had to be big. The biggest. I needed to find the highest platform on Earth from which to share my story and scream out to the world that no matter how bad things may seem, no matter how dire the situation, there is always, always hope. I needed to show people that anything is possible when you harness the amazing power of your mind.

That's when it came to me: What if I climbed Mt. Everest? Me. A guy with one lung. A guy who had beaten the odds and cancer—twice! A guy from Willard, Ohio, scale the world's tallest mountain! Now that would be inspiring. That would give people hope.

The thing was . . . was it even physically possible?

There was only one way to find out.

PART II
The Top of the World

By Sean Swarner

Chapter 4

Mom and Dad had moved down from Ohio to South Carolina in order to be closer to Seth and me, but about a year later, we broke it to them that we were packing up the car and moving to Colorado so I could train to climb Mt. Everest. You can imagine how well that went over.

My parents, who had always been supportive of me, told me they thought I was a lunatic for even attempting something like this. I had zero training, zero experience, zero knowledge, zero gear—zip! Nada! Nothing! Okay, maybe they had a point.

The one thing I did have, however, was a steadfast belief in myself and in the philosophy that if I truly wanted something and put my entire being into it, I could achieve anything. My parents still thought I was crazy, but, like I said, they had always been supportive and encouraged me to push myself, to follow my heart. So they wished me well and gave me their blessing.

Thinking about what I wanted to accomplish was almost overwhelming. I literally had everything going against me. For starters, I was planning on climbing the highest mountain on Earth, yet I lived in a state that's more or less just one, big, table-flat sand bar. The highest point in Florida, for crying out loud, is the top of the Four Seasons Hotel in Miami. On top of that, there was so much I had to think about as far as training, funding (climbing Everest isn't exactly free, you know), gear, climbing skills, etc. The list seemed never-ending.

So I decided I was going to have to tackle this challenge the same way I did everything else in my life: I was going to picture myself on top and successful before I even began. It worked for my cancers, it worked for my swimming, it worked for other areas in my life, and I had no reason to believe it wouldn't work for this. I would start at the end—at the summit of Everest—and then work backwards. That way I would be able to picture what I needed to do and then figure out how to make it happen. Visualizing myself on the summit would enable my mind to research the necessary steps and then prepare me, mentally, to make it happen.

That night, as I lay down to sleep, I used the tools and techniques I learned from countless books on visualization. I slowly breathed in to relax my body, but more importantly, my mind. A few deep breaths through my stomach, and then I began the relaxation by curling my toes and engaging the muscles in my feet. Slowly I'd work up to my calves, then to my quads and hamstrings, then to my glutes, then to my stomach muscles, and all the way up my body to the top of my head until every muscle was tense. Then, with a long, slow exhale, I released all that tension, all the anxiety, and pictured my body like a puddle of Jell-O. I repeated this technique at least ten times until my body was completely relaxed and my mind wasn't running a million miles a minute. If thoughts floated into my mind, I just let them come in and float away again, so that my mind could focus on what was really important: reaching the summit of the highest mountain in the world.

Working backwards from the summit, the first and most obvious thing I needed to do was train. Of course, I couldn't do this in Florida. I needed to go someplace where there were hills. Big ones. My research told me that place was Estes Park, Colorado.

There wasn't a dry eye around as Seth and I packed up my Honda Civic, a.k.a. Pepe, said our goodbyes, and began our cross-country journey. We had no jobs, barely any savings, and not one sponsor to help finance this very expensive, yet monumental adventure. Basically, we had no direction. Neither of us had ever done anything like this before.

Actually, no one in the world had attempted to do what I was about to do. Let that sink in for a moment. There are over seven *billion* people on Earth, and in the entire history of human existence, no other cancer survivor, let alone two-time cancer survivor, with just one functioning lung, had ever attempted to climb Mt. Everest. Honestly, I had no idea how I was going to do it myself. All I knew was that I was going to find a way to make it happen. After all, I had already been to the summit—at least, in my mind.

Before Seth and I had left for Colorado, I managed to procure some lodging once we got there. And by *lodging*, I mean a camp site. Yep, a dirt patch. My bed was a sleeping bag on top of a sleeping pad. For the next month and a half, we lived out of a tent and made our meals by campfire. Essentially, we were homeless. Conditions were pretty much horrible, as you can imagine, but we made the best it and met a lot of great people from all over the states.

My office at the time consisted of a payphone at the camp site and the computers at the library. I knew I needed gear for the trip and that I needed to find sponsorship. Unfortunately, just about every company I approached slammed the door in my face. Most of them just came out and told me that what I was attempting was physically impossible. It just wasn't going to happen. One famous author, who shall remain nameless, actually said to me, "Eight months in Estes Park does not a Himalayan climber make." Most people just thought I was crazy.

I was definitely getting frustrated. But I always kept pushing forward. Remember, in my mind's eye I was already successful and standing on top of the world.

Just when things looked hopeless, one company finally said yes. My determination and perseverance had paid off! Now that we had some backing, it was time to focus on the physical part. If I was going to do something that no one in history had ever done before, it would take a level of training and effort never seen before.

In Colorado, there are a number of mountains called "14ers" i.e., ones that rise above 14,000 feet. There was actually one right in my backyard in Rocky Mountain National Park called Long's Peak. It's 14,256 feet tall, and roughly eighteen miles, round trip, from the base to the top. This was my training ground. Eventually I worked my way up to climbing the mountain around once a week with 100 pounds of rocks in my backpack. I figured if I could carry 100 pounds of rocks up 14,000 feet, I could definitely carry thirty pounds of oxygen to 29,000 feet. In order to get my body used to the cold, I would hike Long's Peak wearing shorts. Many times I would go gloveless and attempt to hike with snowballs in my hands. The way I saw it, I couldn't do enough to prepare myself to scale the highest mountain on Earth.

Evergreens on Fall River, a satellite cabin rental establishment in Estes Park, had heard about my battles and my goal to climb Everest, and were gracious enough to offer us their downstairs apartment. In exchange, we would help on their property by cleaning the cabins, clearing snow, and basically anything else they needed. It was a blessing, to say the least. After a couple of months of camping out in the elements, Seth and I finally had a roof over our heads and a kitchen in which to make proper meals. We finally had our "base camp," if you will.

I knew I was going to be spending a lot of time alone on Everest. While most expeditions have as many as fifty people, including clients, guides, cooks, porters, etc., mine would only have five: a cook, my brother as the Base Camp coordinator, two Sherpas, and myself. Knowing this, I spent many days going up and down the mountains alone. I'd gather up my backpack, with my tent strapped to the outside, some food, a sleeping bag and pad, and other random things I needed for a night out in the mountains by myself, I'd toss everything into the Civic and made my way to the trailhead.

Before leaving, I'd always head into the bathroom to look at myself one last time. Putting my hands on the sides of the sink, I'd look into the mirror and read the yellow Post-It notes with things written on them like "Sponsorship," "Training," "Focus," and "Enjoy the Journey." At the top of the mirror, in all capitals, was one word: "EVEREST." I read those every day to remind me of what I was doing and to keep me focused on the ultimate goal.

During one of these solo expeditions, the roads were pretty clear, but off to each side were mountains of snow stacked five feet high. Timing it just right, I pulled into the parking lot near the trailhead right as the sun was setting. I knew everyone was off the mountain by that point, because mine was the only car in sight. I tossed on my heavy pack and headed up into the darkness, my headlamp lighting the way.

I pushed forward through the windy night for a couple hours, my light reflecting off of the white snow, only my thoughts to keep me company. Although I tried to focus only on positive, affirmative thoughts, every now and then a negative one would slip through the cracks, i.e., *What the [explicative] are you doing?* Undaunted, I'd recognize it, but then let it slide through, say hello, but not allow it to grow roots in my mind.

I kept plodding forward through knee-deep snow until I found a small opening in the trees that was relatively flat and the perfect size for my tent. Plopping my backpack down, the silence and overwhelming sensation of aloneness was powerfully frightening.

There are monsters in the woods that will eat me!

Calm down, Sean. Nothing is going to bother you. Besides, it's too cold for anything to be out here now.

This inner-banter continued back and forth and kept me entertained while I set up my fabric domicile.

Modern tents are pretty simple to put up. Inside each of the aluminum supportive tubes are bungee cords that are attached to each end of a group of ten or so smaller tubes. Once the tubes are locked together end to end, they form a long, flexible stick that gets inserted into a sleeve on the outside of the tent. When these are in place, you push them up, which in turn pulls the tent up. At least that's the way it's supposed to work.

As I began to put the smaller tubes together, I noticed something wasn't right, and the bungee cords weren't pulling as tightly as normal. In fact, they weren't doing anything at all. Grabbing two sections and pulling on the bungee cord on the inside to make it shorter, and thus helping the shorter sections come together in their sleeves, they still weren't staying in place. There was just no tension because it was so cold. I kept forcing them together one piece at a time until I got to the last of the smaller tubes and noticed at least four inches of bungee sticking out of the second to last tube. I tried shoving it into the final section, but there was just too much of it. I couldn't get the full length of the cord into the tubes and, therefore, I couldn't get the full length of the structure to make the tent pop up. I tried another section of poles. Same problem. Another set: ditto.

I shouted into the darkness, cursing myself for not testing these things at home first.

By now, the night had become frigid, somewhere around twenty below zero. I could tell by the sound of the crunching of the snow. In negative temperatures, when you step on snow it sounds like you're walking on Styrofoam. I had to make a decision—fast. I had already gone through every other pole, and I didn't have a knife to cut the bungee and force the poles together. In all honesty, I didn't want to break the expensive tent. The way I saw it, I had two options: A) pack up and head home, or B) dig a snow cave and hope I survived the night.

I went with option A.

I was so angry with myself. My training and research had taught me to be ready for anything and everything, but I didn't even have enough sense to test out my own gear before heading out into the field on a real adventure. I knew better than that.

As the winds picked up and the temperature continued to fall, I shoved everything I could back into my backpack and headed back down the mountain. The snow had been falling harder and harder, and my footprints, which I was hoping to follow back down to my car, were quickly disappearing. My stomach sank. This was bad.

I started moving faster, which in turn increased my body temperature. And there it was: a bead of sweat dripping down my nose. That might not sound like a big deal, but when the temperature is that low and your body starts sweating, you can quickly fall victim to hypothermia. If I stopped at this point, my sweat would literally freeze on my clothes, and eventually on me, causing my body temperature plummet.

I began to panic. "I can't die out here! I can't die out here! I can't die out here!" Then suddenly what I was saying hit me, and that I needed to flip it around to try and be positive, just like I had been training myself. "I'm going to make it . . . I'm going to make it . . . I *will* make it!"

I continued down the mountain along the snow-covered trail. Scary tree figures watched my every move as I scanned the darkness, making sure no wolves were stalking me for a midnight snack. I started laughing at myself. What fool would go into the mountains, alone, on a freezing cold night without first testing his gear? Talk about stupid. Maybe I'm just not cut out for this. Then, just as the doubt tried to creep back in, the image of Everest popped into my mind, and once again I saw myself standing on top, the curvature of the Earth stretching out before me.

Suddenly something caught my eye to my right. A reflection off of something. Initially it scared the crap out of me, but when I looked back in that direction, my headlamp caught the reflection of...my license plate! I made it back! And I was extremely lucky too, because my footprints had completely disappeared by that point, and I had been going in what I hoped was the right direction. Thankfully I followed my instincts and found Pepe!

Never again did I go into the mountains without first testing and knowing my gear inside and out. Lesson learned, albeit the hard way.

New Year's Day came quickly, and I only had three more months to train before leaving for Nepal and Everest. I had always heard about this group of people who call themselves the Polar Bear Club. If you're not familiar with it, every New Year's Day these crazy folks jump into a body of freezing cold water—a lake, pond, river, etc.—just for the thrill of it. They call it the Polar Bear Plunge. Some get in and swim around, and others just plunge in and pop back out. I've always been up for adventure, and since I thought it might help prepare me the extreme cold on Everest, I thought I'd give it try.

So, on New Year's morning, Seth and I hopped in Pepe and headed out to Lake Estes for our own, private Polar Bear Plunge. Along the way the heat was blasting through the vents. We wanted to be sweating by the time we arrived so the water wouldn't feel as cold. Or at least that's what we hoped.

As soon as we got to the lake, I hopped out with my ice ax and began to chop through the thick blanket of frozen water. Unfortunately, the ice was so hard that I didn't even make a dent. We had to come up with another plan.

Standing on the frozen lake, I looked around for a better spot. Back in the corner of the lake, I could see a little pebble beach-like ramp that led into the cold, black water. Bingo. We jumped back inside Pepe and headed over.

As we pulled up to this new location, we could see that the ice was much thinner and that it probably wouldn't take much chipping to break through to the water below. Keeping the car running and the heat blasting, we jumped out into the cold in our swim suits, wrapped in huge beach towels, with no shoes on our feet. Two morons in their swim suits about to jump into a frozen Colorado lake on freezing cold and snowy January morning. This was nuts.

The initial toe test wasn't too bad, although, that's probably because my feet were frozen from walking on the ice-cold rocks. At first, I tried to ease myself in, but quickly realized that wasn't an option. So I started walking a little faster until I was about mid-thigh, pausing momentarily because I knew what part of my body was next (the part every guy cringes even thinking about). By the time I got to my belly button, I knew I couldn't last much longer, so I took a deep breath and went all in. It literally took my breath away.

I bolted up and out of the frigid water and spewed the air out, instantly gasping for more as I tried to catch my breath. Then the cold air hit my wet skin, and I waddled back to the car as quickly as possible, grabbing my towel from Seth. It was his turn now, but after watching me do it, he didn't exactly look too eager. I jumped into the passenger seat and tried to warm up, but all I could feel were my toes being blasted by the hot air coming out of the vents, which felt like a blow torch. Then, I watched as Seth submerged himself and immediately popped up. The look on his face one of excruciating pain.

Was it horrible? My goodness, yes. It hurt like *you know what*! Would I do it again? You bet I would!

With my scheduled date of departure just a couple months off, it was time to get things organized, packed up, and, most importantly, paid for.

Over the past year, I had done everything I needed to do in order to prepare myself physically. By now I was running up and down the Colorado mountains, jogging to the tops of the 14ers with no problem. I was ready.

My mind was ready, too. I had visualized myself on the summit hundreds, if not thousands of times. The crunching snow, the smell of ozone, the blinding sun, the freezing temperatures—it was all there in my mind, all so real to me. I had seen the summit so many times, and I truly believed with every fiber of my being that it was going to happen.

I had support from sponsors to get my gear. I had put together a training plan that helped me get my body in shape. I had done research on the mountain, spoken to people who had been there, and tried to get as much information as possible about the expedition. I had done everything I needed to do in order to prepare myself for this challenge of a lifetime.

Everything, that is, except raise enough money to pay for it.

As I mentioned before, most people didn't believe it was physically possible for someone to climb Everest with one lung. Because of that, it had been difficult finding the financial support to make the trip possible. When the time came to pay the expedition company, I simply didn't have the money. I was able to talk them down in price somewhat, but it wasn't enough. Still, I was passionate and determined, and I wasn't about to give up now.

When I was born, my parents had put some money into a stock account with reinvesting shares. By this point those shares had been sitting there appreciating for twenty-seven years. It was my only option—I sold every one of them. I even sold some other things online, and still just barely had enough to make the payment.

I had literally invested everything I had into this adventure—mind, body, spirit, and all of my money. There was only one thing left to do.

It was time to climb Mt. Everest.

Chapter 5

I felt a hard thump as the plane's wheels touched down on the runway. I couldn't believe it—I was really here, in Kathmandu, Nepal.

I had never been this far away from home before—twelve time zones away from my home in Colorado. I was nervous, but also excited. I had worked so hard to get to this moment, and it had been such an adventure just to get here. Little did I know the extent of the adventure that lay before me.

Back in South Carolina, roughly 12,000 miles away, Mom and Dad were sitting at home praying for their first-born son and hoping that he'd come back alive. "Look," they had said to me before I left, "we didn't get you through two cancers just so you could go off and kill yourself on a hunk of rock and ice."

Parents. Always worrying about something. What can you do?

When they opened the doors to let us off the plane, I nearly choked on the heavily, polluted air that came rushing into the cabin. It was as if the plane had taken a big long drag of a cig-arette. I stepped off and looked around at the thick smog and glowing orange lights piercing through it. A feeling of relief swept over me. I had nothing more to worry about, that is, except getting my back side up the tallest mountain on the planet. No sweat.

I had just stepped off a plane into a strange city that I was sure was going to give me cancer for the third time, but I had come this far, I wasn't going to let a little smog get in my way. After all, I was here to make history. Deep down I was already on the summit, already successful. A warm smile grew across my face. I could see the white snow. I could feel the icy wind blowing across my face. I could hear the sound of the glacier crunching beneath my boots' metal spikes. I could feel someone nudging me from behind . . .

"Oh, sorry about that," I said, emerging from my daydream and nearly falling down the steps from the plane. I knew I was in the right place. This was where I was meant to be. Everything was all right in Sean World again.

Fortunately my brother Seth had joined me on this adven-ture, and after we checked into our hotel, we started going through my gear for the expedition. The initial plan had been for him to climb Everest alongside me in order to demonstrate the importance of family support through adversity, but the tre-mendous cost of this endeavor made that impossible. Although he wasn't going to be my climbing partner, he was still going to play a big role in my expedition as my Base Camp coordinator. Most importantly, he would be my eyes and ears when I made it into the "Death Zone"—an altitude where the human body literally starts deteriorating.

The local high-altitude guides, a.k.a. Sherpas, that I was going to climb with—Kame and Nima Gombu—had both done Everest before. What's funny is, they were actually nervous about meeting me. You see, it's very rare that someone survives cancer in Nepal. So when they came into our hotel room, they were relieved to see someone who was the picture of health. Looking at me, you'd never know that I had a terrible disease twice, or that I had just one lung. Thanks to all my hard work, I was in tremendous shape and more than ready to do this thing.

As they looked through my gear, Kame and Nima Gombu were happy with everything except for one thing—my boots. They didn't like my boots and said that they weren't good enough to climb past the last camp to the summit. They weren't warm enough. If I wanted to come home with my toes still attached to my feet, I needed to get the right kind of boots.

I turned to Seth. "Dude," I said, "I'm 6'2". The average Nepali guy is, what, Maybe 5'5"? Where are we going to find size thirteen boots in two days?"

We both started laughing. What else could we do? This was Kathmandu, where everyone begins their journey to Everest. Surely there had to be at least one pair of size thirteen boots somewhere in the city. At least that's what we were hoping.

So the next day we took off into the great unknown of Kathmandu. Incredibly, we found pair of size thirteen boots—the right kind of boots—at an expedition store. In fact, not only did they have boots, they had down summit suits, mittens, and basically everything you would ever need to get up the mountain. The boots were a horrible fluorescent yellow, which I found out would be very handy should something happen on the mountain and they had to locate me. It would be a stark contrast against the white snow, and they could find my body easier. What a pleasant thought. They were used boots, and the previous owner apparently wore them during a successful climb the previous year. *Sweet!* I thought. *Lucky boots!* I could just hear the summit calling my name.

The Kathmandu locals have a saying: "The clouds have mountains." They told me that it was very dangerous flying into Lukla, the town where I was to begin my trek to Everest Base Camp. But honestly, I had no other choice. So once again Seth and I found ourselves back at the Kathmandu Airport, hauling our bags and my gear through the terminal. Grabbing the heavy duffels, I tossed them onto the scale (which was way off, by the way) so they could get tagged and loaded into the back of the tiny, twelve-seater that would fly us to the beginning of our adventure. As I walked through the metal detector before boarding, I looked down and—and I kid you not—the thing wasn't even plugged in!

Our plane didn't exactly instill me with confidence either. The front looked all burnt from the prop engines and the seats were all worn and torn. It looked as if it had been through World War II. (Who knows, maybe it had?) I had to bend over just to get inside, and working my way to my seat near the front I thought I might break my back. A quick cough of the engine, a nasty black plume of smoke, the smell of burning oil, and the propeller engines slowly kicked into action. *Everest, here we come!*

After bouncing around on the tarmac, somehow the old plane managed to lift off as we headed into the Nepalese sky. Looking out my yellow-tinted window, I could see mountain peaks rising up through a sea of clouds. It was one of the most amazing views I had ever seen. The vastness of the landscape left me awestruck, and suddenly any worries I had about smacking nose-first into the side of a mountain drifted away.

Soaring above the snow-covered peaks, I began to dream about Everest and see myself standing atop the summit of the world. Emotion swept over me as I thought of everything I had gone through to get here and why I was doing it. I didn't fight the feelings. The more emotional I could make this event, the more attachment I had to it, the more able I would be to deal with whatever adversity and hardships awaited me. The same mental image that had inspired over the past year of training once again came to mind, and I could see the world dropping off in front of me and stretching out as far as the eye could see. It was a warm, wonderful feeling.

Until, that is, I was jolted back to reality when the plane abruptly dropped in altitude and I got that roller-coaster feeling in the pit of my stomach as we descended rapidly to the tiny airport in the middle of the Himalayas.

"That thing can't be the airport," I said to my brother. Up ahead, between the shoulders of the pilots in front of us, the landing strip stretched out into the distance like a thin piece of black electrical tape. I wasn't too worried until I noticed that missing the runway meant certain death. If we came in too fast and too hard, we would end up running smack into the side of a mountain. If we came up short, we'd find ourselves plummeting down the side of the cliff. As it turns out, Lukla has the dubious distinction of being the world's most dangerous airport. Wonderful.

Knowing I had zero control over what happened, I figured I may as well enjoy my last moments on Earth and do what any other sane person would do in this circumstance—get it on video, of course! I pulled out my camera and hoped for the best as we made our approach. Moments later the wheels thwacked down on the runway and everyone on board lurched forward as the pilots slammed on the brakes to avoid smacking into the Himalyas directly ahead of us.

Once again, I turned to Seth. "Well," I said, "let the adventure begin!"

Hunching over with my backpack strapped over my shoulders, I made my way to the door at the back of the plane. I stuck my head out of the door and smiled. Here I was, just an average, Midwestern guy, about to embark on an historic climb to the summit of Mt. Everest. Unbelievable.

Getting to Everest Base Camp takes about fourteen days. (Coincidentally, that's the same number of days I was given to live the second time I was diagnosed with cancer.) It's only about a fifty-mile trek, but the higher you go in altitude, the less atmospheric pressure there is on your body. If you go too high too fast, you could succumb to High Altitude Cerebral Edema

(HACE) or High-Altitude Pulmonary Edema (HAPE)—both serious and potentially lethal illnesses. With cerebral edema, what basically happens is your brain swells. In case you didn't notice, your brain is encased in a pretty solid, protective shell, a.k.a. your skull. If your gray matter starts swelling, the pressure builds up in your brain, you go unconscious, and you die. With pulmonary edema, liquid collects in your lungs, and eventually you end up drowning on your own fluids. Neither is an ideal way to go, so you definitely want to take your time getting up there.

I was fortunate to be with experienced people who had been to the top before. My new friend Pemba actually had family in Lukla. This was key because my gear had to find its way to Base Camp somehow, and I sure wasn't going to carry two large duffel bags full of climbing gear for fifty miles. Through Pemba, we were able to hire a Sherpa and a Sherpani (a female Sherpa) who had some yaks that could carry all of our gear to the base of Everest.

After hiring the porter Sherpas and their yaks, we made our way through Lukla and out of town to begin our journey.

Yaks, by the way, aren't exactly the brightest of animals. In the Sherpa culture, the yak is considered one of the dumbest creatures on the face of the Earth. If you've never seen one before, imagine a cross between a cow and a goat. Add on lots and lots of long, furry hair, and give it some big horns that make it top-heavy. Oh, and don't forget a bell that constantly dings with every single step. Because they were hauling all of my gear up to Everest Base Camp, these quirky creatures quickly became my best friends.

We passed through a lot of villages along the way to Base Camp, and the people in these little towns were incredibly friendly and welcoming. Tourists are their bread and butter, so they rely on people like myself to show up year after year to stay in their houses, camp in their yards, or stop in for a bite to eat. Trekkers from around the world stop in for a warm cup of tea and to shake off the deep chill.

Hiking along the dirt trail, taking in the most amazing views I had ever seen in my life, I felt both exhilarated and anxious. Sure, I had trained in the Rockies in Colorado, but those mountains were mole hills compared to the Himalayas. Keeping an eye out for the jumping rocks that seemed to be all over the trail (rocks that magically jumped up, caught my shoes, and made me trip), we hiked higher and higher. Off to my left I could hear sound of the glacial-fed river rushing by and down the mountain. Taking in the views of the lush, green mountainsides that surrounded me, I felt like I was being welcomed into the Himalayas with open arms.

Then, off in the distance, I noticed a couple people walking across what appeared to be a bridge spanning the noisy river. The mountain came to an abrupt stop at a cliff that fell hundreds of feet to the racing white water below. The bridge seemed to come out of the side of the rock face to the left and then, after crossing the span, was somehow anchored to the other side of the mountain. Above it rose a majestic peak covered in pine trees, reminding me of Colorado.

Slowly, we approached the makeshift bridge. Grabbing a rock lodged in the ground with one hand and a tree root with the other, I pulled myself up the trail that kept getting steeper as we went. Ahead of me stretched out the approximately 500-foot-long span. Plank after plank of wooden two-by-fours were connected to two metal cables that stretched across the entire width of the river valley. On top of the cables, a grid of metal straps ran from one side of the bridge to the other. Attached to both the planks and the cables was what looked like regular chain-link fencing.

Up until this point, Seth and I had been cruising along and having a great time on the trail, but when we came to this so-called "bridge," we stopped dead. As I mentioned before, yaks aren't very smart, but even they stopped when they came to this bridge, which made me think that maybe they're not that stupid after all. As I looked over the side, where it dropped down to the raging river hundreds of feet below, I couldn't help but think of that scene in "Indiana Jones and the Temple of Doom," where they had to cross a bridge just like this one, and it collapsed, sending people falling to their deaths in the crocodile-infested river below. Hopefully things would turn out better for us.

Without wasting any more time, I launched myself onto the bridge, completely carefree. I began running, stomping, and jumping until the cables started to sway up and down, creating a wave in the makeshift platform. Our guides must have thought I was crazy. (And maybe they're right.) I turned around and smiled at Seth, who had a huge grin on his face, too. When I reached the other side, I turned around and did it again, just for the heck of it. Then back to the other side and back again. I felt like a kid at the playground. It was awesome! I was on the adventure of a lifetime, and I planned on enjoying every single moment.

As we continued on up the path, at one point I looked up, and above my head hung an old, splintered, wooden sign welcoming me to Namche Bazaar. This would be our home for the next couple of nights.

After checking in to our "hotel" and grabbing some dinner, I headed to my room to lie down and practice my visualization of being at the summit. Eventually I fell asleep, a large, contented smile across my face. Tomorrow was going to be another day and another adventure.

Chapter 6

KAPOW!
    I was jolted out of bed by something incredibly loud and not too far away.

KAPOW! There it was again. Over in the other bed next to me, Seth sat straight up and looked at me, a frightened, bewildered look on his face.

"Rifles!" I said, "Someone's out there shooting rifles!" I held my breath and listened, thoughts racing through my mind. *Should we leave? Should we hide?* The silence was deafening as my brother and I stared out into the darkness and waited. Five minutes passed. Then ten. Fifteen. Eventually we lay back down again, thinking the danger was over, until . . .

KAPOW! Another shot! This time it sounded even closer. Once again, I bolted upright in the darkness, terrified. And then . . . silence.

I have no idea when or how I managed to fall back asleep, but when I woke up the next morning, I strolled downstairs to the common area where I found people chatting and talking about the noises from the previous night. Approaching the owner of the establishment, I asked him if he knew anything about the gunshots. Apparently, they really were rifle shots, but that's not the scary part. What really freaked me out was that they were shots fired by Maoists—and they were looking for Americans! Wonderful. As if making my way up the highest mountain in the world, with one lung, wasn't dangerous enough. Now I had to dodge American-hating terrorists, too.

The owner could see how worried I was, but he assured me that the Maoists weren't really that close to Namche and that I was safe. They were down lower in the villages and most likely on their way to Kathmandu. This eased my mind somewhat as we headed out to explore a little higher up in the village, where I'd heard the view was absolutely amazing.

As we crested the ridge outside of town, the view grew more spectacular with every step. It was hands down the most amazing sight my eyes had ever seen. Off in the distance, the unimaginably tall mountains of the Himalayas rose into the sky, covered in pristine white, glacial snow and ice. The stark contrast of the blue sky against the white mountainside was mesmerizing, and the vastness of it all took my breath away.

My eyes traced the peaks on the horizon, one after another, until something in the distance caught my eye. Something I had been dreaming about every night for the past eight months. She was unmistakable, with her telltale snow plume blowing horizontally off the summit. There she was: Everest. Tall, strong, and proud. I pictured myself on the summit countless times, and now there she was, looking right back at me. Calling to me.

Knowing I'd be at the base in about a week, I smiled and whispered, "I'll see you soon."

Chapter 7

After another night in Namche—this time quiet with no gunshots—we continued our journey ever higher into the Himalayas.

The next day we arrived in a town called Chukhung. I was surrounded by the highest mountains in the world, and it was breathtaking. The valley was so large it could easily hold the entire island of Manhattan. Because of the altitude, the vegetation had completely disappeared, and the entire valley was dirt brown. Sitting inside the common area of the local hostel, I was writing in my journal about the day's hike. In the middle of the room sat an iron heater, a staple of every home at this altitude. People were gathered close around it, sitting in plastic chairs as they warmed their feet and dried their socks. A small chimney attached to the top guided the smoke up and out of the top of the building. Just outside lay rows of round, squished brown patties with undigested hay sticking out of the sides. Dung chips. Yak patties. Whatever you want to call them, they served as fuel for the fire. With no wood this high up, the locals had to make do with what was available and burned them to heat the room.

The common area was loaded with people from around the globe. They were reading, writing, talking, playing cards—whatever would help pass the time. Part of getting your body used to the altitude is resting once you arrive at your destination. It's only about fifty miles from Lukla to Everest Base Camp, but when you're on this pilgrimage to the tallest mountain in the world, you need to take your time. Doing so helps the body produce more red blood cells and hemoglobin, which can prevent it from succumbing to those serious high-altitude issues.

There are different issues that can affect the human body in higher altitudes. There's the typical AMS (Acute Mountain Syndrome), where you feel nauseous, dizzy, and short of breath (you may even vomit). Then there are the more severe issues like HACE (brain swelling) and HAPE (drowning on bodily fluids). In addition, there's also less oxygen, about one-third less. If it were possible for someone to go directly to the summit of Everest without letting their body adjust gradually, that person would die in in a matter of minutes. Because of this, climbers exercise extreme caution, taking their time so their bodies can adjust. Some people take their time, and still their body doesn't adjust for one reason or another. Every time the human body goes into altitude again, and it's not acclimatized, it can act differently. It's a crap shoot, really.

In just a few days I would be stumbling into Base Camp and my new home for the next month and a half. With a huge mountain like Everest, you don't just arrive at Base Camp and then push for the summit. I was going to have to establish four different camps along the way, hauling my gear up and down the mountain to get my body used to the altitude. Once again, I was going to be living inside a tent for over a month, except this time on the side of a mountain, and not in a camp site in Colorado. Anyone not willing to go at least a few weeks without showering need not apply.

By the time dinner rolled around, I was craving meat, so I ordered the yak burger. I know, it's horrible. Here I was eating the meat of the same animals (well, not the exact same animals) that were hauling my gear up the mountain for me. But in Nepal it's a staple of their diet. That and something called dal bhat, which essentially is a mixture of rice, lentils, and their own unique combination of spices and flavoring. I had eaten dal bhat at lunch and dinner for the past ten days, and I was ready for something else, something with substance—like a big, fat, juicy yak burger!

I wish I could say I bit into it and it melted in my mouth, but instead it was hard, chewy, and honestly not very tasty. But hey, I wasn't going to complain. It was meat and it was what my body needed.

Looking back, maybe I should have passed on the yak burger, because the next day while I was hiking, a train of yaks loaded with gear was going past me and one by one they all stepped on my foot.

Karma's a bit—.

With only about a day left of trekking to Base Camp, we were approaching a little bump in the trail, and eerily perched on the ridge a few hundred feet in front me stood a dozen dark apparitions. They grew larger and larger the closer we hiked, and the awesome sight of them gave me goosebumps. Made of shale and other rocks from around the area, these rectangular shapes stood about six or seven feet tall. Between them, and strung from the top of one to the other, flew tattered and sun-bleached prayer flags. A shiver ran up my spine as I cautiously walked between the stone giants, noticing that there were more of them continuing down on each side of the trail. They were all unique in shape but still very similar to the others. Some were massive with more flags, while others were made of only a few rocks stacked on top of one another. And each featured a plaque with an inscription on it. They were all so beautiful, so why did I have this strange, unsettled feeling in my stomach?

As I approached one of the smaller ones for a closer inspection, suddenly it hit me: These weren't trail-side decorations for tourists hiking by; they were memorials, markers meant to honor someone who had died on Everest. And there were literally hundreds of them. Hundreds of people who had lost their lives doing what I was about to attempt.

Walking through this mountaintop cemetery, I was reminded of the reason I had embarked on this journey in the first place: to inspire people touched by cancer. How many people had been affected or taken by this horrible, merciless disease? It made me think of how, in a way, we are all kindred spirits, all striving to reach our goals in life, all trying to find our way to the top of our own personal Everest.

These stone memorials served as a sobering reminder that what I was about to attempt may kill me. I had thought about death many times and had come to terms with my own mortality. But when it's actually staring you right in the face, it's completely different. It all becomes so real. I thought about all the souls on the mountain. All the people in the world who had been touched by cancer. All the people who were currently battling disease. The incredible weight of it all hit me in the chest and knocked the wind out of me. I was reminded of the hardships in my life and what I had gone through to get to this point. It was crazy to think of everything I had lived through and to try and understand where my life was headed. I had always felt that I was just plodding along in life with no real direction, and that everything was just happening around me. But as I stood among the stones, looking back at my life I realized that every step I had taken was a choice. Every decision I had made, every turn I had taken, had brought me to where I was right now, on my way to the top of the world.

Chapter 8

Everest—a name synonymous with majesty, mystery, and greatness . . . but also with misery and death.

At its peak, the world's tallest mountain is nearly six miles above sea level. It's one of the most inhospitable places on the planet, and scaling it is one of the most difficult challenges anyone can face. Human beings just aren't made to survive in such thin air, at the same altitude jumbo jets fly. Just above Base Camp, helicopters are actually unable fly because the air is so thin—there's nothing for the rotors to bite into to create lift. Those lucky few climbers who manage to make it to the windy, frigid, icy summit are surviving out of sheer will, determination, and mental toughness.

It was like nothing I'd ever seen or experienced before. Standing among the rocky outcroppings and frozen stalagmites of ice all around Base Camp, 17,600 feet up, I breathed in the incredibly thin, bone-chilling air and thought about spending the next forty-five days here—in a tent. For the next month and a half I was actually going to be living in a tent on top of a glacier that was moving four feet a day. Four feet a day! Every morning I woke up at Base Camp I was going to be four feet further from my goal. Talk about frustrating!

The past eight months of my life had been dedicated to training and research and getting my mind and body ready for the most difficult challenge on Earth. I had been up and down some of the tallest peaks in the lower forty-eight states, multiple times. I knew I had done everything I needed to do in order to face Everest. But when I actually stood in its shadow, I truly felt how tiny and insignificant I was.

It's hard to understand how incomprehensibly large Everest is. You know that quintessential photo of the mountain, the one with the snow plume blowing horizontally off the summit? Well, that plume is actually caused by the summit puncturing the jet stream, and at times blowing well over 200 miles per hour. Here, avalanches occur on a daily basis, at least a dozen times a day. Rocks the size of cars tumble down the sides of the mountain and can be heard for miles. Temperatures range anywhere from eighty-five above to eighty below zero, and can drop from eighty to zero in as little as five minutes. This is because at this altitude you're literally closer to the sun and the radiation is more intense because there's less atmosphere to filter the intense rays. If clouds get in front of the sun, the temperature absolutely plummets. The next time you're on a passenger plane and the captain says over the speakers, "We've reached our cruising altitude of 29,000 feet . . . sit back and enjoy your flight," look out the window—and up another thirty-five feet. That's how massive Everest is.

Sherpas believe the mountain is a goddess. They call her either Chomolungma or Sagarmatha, meaning "mother goddess of the universe." Because of this, you aren't allowed to just show up and start climbing. My climbing group (like every other expedition on the mountain)—which included me and my two Sherpas, Kame and Ang Dorgee—had to get permission from the mountain before heading up. I suppose if I were a mountain goddess, I'd want people to ask permission to climb up me, too.

We had to go through what's called a Puja Ceremony, where a Lama (i.e., a spiritual leader in Tibetan Buddhism; not the furry, four-legged animal that spits) speaks to the mountain through chants, incantations, the burning of incense and sage, and lots and lots of drinking a type of a tangy rice beer called chhaang. From what I've been told, in order to speed up the fermentation process, while the women are sitting around the pot stirring the chhaang, they spit in it. Yum! That might explain the funky tang.

Anyhow, during this Puja ceremony, the Lama chants and communicates with the mountain, asking for permission to climb her and for safe passage. As I sat there taking it all in, I thought to myself, *this is interesting . . . I just spent eight grueling months training, flew 12,000 miles around the world, spent fourteen days hiking fifty-some miles to get to Base Camp, and sold just about everything I owned in order to fund this expedition. Now here I am waiting for some dude to get permission from a mountain so I can climb. Awesome.*

I turned and asked my Sherpa friend if the mountain ever said no. He smiled and said, "Yes, many times."

Even better.

"So what happens then?" I asked. I was told we'd have to have a new Puja ceremony and get a new Lama to perform the ceremony. But that wasn't the kicker. With the new Lama, we'd pay him even more money. Seriously?

So after a lot of chanting, chhaang drinking, fire burning, and waiting, the mountain granted us permission to climb her. Looks like we paid the first Lama enough money. Thank God. (Or more appropriately, thank goddess.)

Climbing up to Base Camp we had taken our time, and it had been relatively easy. But climbing to the summit would be an entirely different experience. In such thin air we would have to establish camps along the way and haul our gear higher and higher up the mountain as we went. Our first task would be to set up Camp One, right around 19,000 feet. But to do that we'd first have to climb through the Khumbu Icefall, the most dangerous section of the climb.

Picture in your mind New York City. Manhattan. Now lean the entire island on an angle enough to make all the buildings domino and collapse onto one another. Now, picture all those fallen skyscrapers as solid chunks of ice, with the largest chunk being roughly the size of the Empire State Building, and all those chunks of ice on a glacier that's moving four feet a day. That's the Khumbu Icefall. Often times the entire pile settles. You know when you have a glass of ice water, and after the water is gone, the ice cubes drop all of a sudden? Now picture that happening on a massive, incomprehensible scale. The sound of the giant ice chunks popping and grinding against one another is a terrifying sound, and it's one I'll never forget.

Our acclimatization period began with our first trip up through the Khumbu Icefall, that first step up the mountain. Rounding skyscraper-sized ice chunks, I didn't quite make Camp One like we'd initially planned. Right around 19,000 feet, I developed a horrible cough that kept slowing me down. Worse yet, I was coughing up blood. Great. Like I didn't have enough things going against me.

Because of the thin air and how easily and quickly it goes in and out of the lungs, many climbers on Everest get something called the Khumbu Cough. It's a horrible, debilitating cough that's so constant, so harsh and violent that people have actually gotten broken ribs from it, as they try to expel the fluid in their lungs. Luckily mine wasn't that violent, but I was certainly getting an abdominal workout.

Returning to Base Camp, I met up with a doctor from one of the neighboring expeditions, and she gave me some antibiotics to help curb whatever infection I was battling. Eventually I was diagnosed with what they thought was bronchitis, which, in that situation, could have killed me. Over time and numerous incredibly difficult trips up the mountain, my body gradually recovered.

My Sherpa friends and I carried our gear in our backpacks through the Icefall and further up the mountain at the established camps. Coming back down wasn't too difficult since our packs were nearly empty. After a rest, we loaded up our packs and head back up the mountain. We needed time for our bodies to acclimatize so we wouldn't suffer from HAPE or HACE, and so that we could be as strong as possible on the push to the summit.

Every time we returned to Base Camp, we would rest to let our bodies manufacture more red blood cells and hemoglobin. That rest period could be a day or two, maybe three or even more. It's a lot like going through chemo, where the human body can't handle another onslaught of treatments until it produces more blood cells, otherwise the treatments can be deadly. It's the same thing here. Each time I went higher in altitude, I had to let my body rest and recover before going any higher.

One night while resting at Base Camp, I laid in my tent and focused again on the image of standing on the summit, fully believing I was already successful. As I drifted off to sleep, I had a dream. It wasn't about reaching the summit, or kissing some hot celebrity however, it was about going to Disney World—with the talking M&Ms from the television commercials. Go figure. We were walking around the amusement park looking for Laffy Taffy.

Oh well. At least I wasn't looking for yak burgers.

Chapter 9

For the next few weeks, I continued to get myself adjusted to higher and higher altitudes. Every step along the way was higher than I had ever been before. It was completely unexplored territory. I had pushed through the onset of bronchitis and had been up and down the mountain about fifteen times, eventually reaching 23,000 feet where we set up Camp Three. My first night there was amazing. I had overcome the constant hacking, thanks to some miracle antibiotics. And no one—and I mean no one—had believed it was physically possible for someone with just one lung to make it past Camp Two. Yet here I was. My mind was sharp. My body was a machine, and I felt unstoppable.

The same group that helped me with the bronchitis was performing tests on climbers and doing research on high altitude cerebral edema. They were testing visual patterns and the mind's ability to differentiate those patterns based on different altitudes, and they asked me to be a subject in their experiments. Basically they were testing the brain's ability to function in extreme altitude with less oxygen. They wanted to learn how the fewer molecules affected the mind's ability to distinguish differences without confusion.

The test consisted of a set of 4x6 cards that flipped up and over like a Rolodex. On one card there would be things like a small triangle, a medium-sized triangle, a larger triangle, and then a square. Others might have four geometric shapes, where three of them had eight sides and one had five. My job was to figure out which one didn't belong and then relay my answer back to the team.

It sounds pretty simple, but when your brain isn't receiving enough oxygen, it can't distinguish even the simplest of differences. It might take thirty seconds to figure out the correct answer, or you could give the wrong answer all together. When you're at 23,000 feet, something a three-year-old would laugh at becomes difficult for a grown adult because the brain is hypoxic and starved for oxygen.

Since I was feeling so great, I decided to have a little fun with them back down at Base Camp. Holding their little Rolodex-type test, I pushed the button my walkie-talkie. "Base Camp, this is Sean. Do you copy?"

"Sean, we copy. How's everything up there?"

"It was a *hot* day today, but I'm up at Camp Three and feeling pretty good. How's everything down there?"

"Same ol', same ol'," they replied. "Wake up, get breakfast, walk around, wait for weather updates, read, journal . . . you know the drill. By the way, Seth's here."

Seth's familiar voice cracked over the radio speaker. "Hey, buddy! How's it going? Feeling okay?"

"Yeah, man. I feel great! Thanks. But I'd like to get this test over with so I can get some dinner and get ready for bed. I want to get some rest before tonight. Probably be difficult to sleep."

"Yeah, probably. Okay, I'll let you guys do your thing. We can talk later. Seven work for you?"

"Copy that, Seth. Talk to you at seven. Okay guys, let me know when you're ready."

"We're all here, Sean. If you want to flip open to the first page and start, then just go through like you did at Camp Two, that would be great."

I smiled. This was going to be fun. Sitting cross-legged in the tent, I picked up the test, walkie-talkie in hand, and pushed the button to begin talking. "Okay, page one, number three, the penguin." Then, flipping to the next set of images, I continued the test. "Page two, number one, the house. Page three, number four, the giraffe."

By this point, I was having a hard time not laughing. I went through a few more pages without letting them talk, and spouted off things like a lion, a whale, the dog, a cat, etc. The thing was, there were no animals on any of the pages. They were all geo-metric shapes.

Finally I lifted my thumb from the talk button and waited for a response. After a *very* long pause, I heard the crack of the radio with them on the other end.

"Um . . . Sean? You feeling okay?"

I quickly responded. "Yeah, great. Why?" Another really long pause followed.

"We're a little concerned about you. You might wanna think about coming back down soon, because . . . well . . . Sean, there are no animals on those pages."

Altitude does weird things to you, and the simplest of things can seem hysterical. I was beside myself laughing as I pushed the button again. "I'm kidding!" I yelled. "I'm just playing with you!"

"Oh, thank goodness!" came the relieved response. "We were *really* worried for a second there."

I'd had my fun, so I restarted the test and did just fine. After a quick dinner, I called it a day and fell asleep for the first time in extreme altitude.

Whenever I was back at Base Camp resting again, I would talk with other hikers and Sherpas, play cards, and even partake in a little chhaang drinking every once in a while. I wanted to enjoy every single moment of this adventure.

One night my brother and I invited a friend of ours named Martine to have dinner with us. It was an amazing meal of authentic Italian pizza, free-range Argentine steak, and fresh vegetables. No, wait—that's what I imagined it to be. In actuality it was just bread covered with shredded carrots and cabbage, ground yak meat, and some boiled potatoes. Regardless, I needed the calories. In extreme altitudes, the body works incredibly hard. Simply to maintain my body weight, I needed roughly 12,000 calories a day, which isn't easy since they don't exactly have fast-food joints on the side of Everest. So I tried to eat as much as possible.

As I was shoveling in the food—I had to eat quickly because it was so cold the food would cool off in a matter of minutes—I noticed Martine was shuffling around in her seat. It was like she couldn't get comfortable or something.

"You okay?" I asked.

"Yes," she answered. "I think I am. I'm fine."

"You sure? You haven't sat still since you came in here."

"Well," she said, "to be honest, my bum doesn't feel right."

I nearly yacked on my yak. "Sorry," I said, "I don't mean to laugh, but that's pretty funny. What's wrong with your butt?"

"I'm not quite sure, but I'm sure it'll be fine." She didn't seem too sure.

"Not to get too personal," I said, "but if you want me to look at it, I can."

"Thanks," she replied. "Maybe tomorrow, if it isn't any better."

Whatever was wrong, it must have been really bothering her, because early the next morning Martine took me up on my offer and asked me if I wouldn't mind "looking at her bum."

You might be wondering how climbers go to the bathroom on the mountain, considering it's so cold. For starters, guys have it *much* easier than the ladies. The hardest thing for males is trying to find "it" through big puffy down pants while wearing huge mittens. It doesn't really leave room for much dexterity. Women, on the other hand, have to unzip most of what they're wearing and, therefore, are more exposed to the elements.

When I looked at Martine's back side, the problem was easy to see—it was lightly frostbitten from having to answer Nature's call during a biting windstorm. *Ouch.* She basically had a frostbitten butt cheek.

But such is life on the mother of all mountains.

When you're climbing Everest, you never know what the day is going to bring. It always seemed like something was going on to challenge me and keep me from reaching the summit.

One day, while coming down from an acclimatization climb up to Camp Two, we stopped to rest in the dangerous Khumbu Icefall. Kame and I were standing on a chunk of ice the size of a school bus, waiting for our turn to descend an aluminum ladder that had been attached to the ice. Often times the terrain is so treacherous you have to put up ladders in order to circumvent it. That was the case here.

There was a lady in front of us going down the ladder. I have no idea where she was from, who she was, or even if she spoke English. All I know is she was taking her good ol' time and being incredibly cautious. I couldn't blame her, considering how slippery metal crampons (spikes attached to boots) can be on a frozen aluminum ladder.

While Kame and I were enjoying our little break and awaiting our turn, suddenly we heard that all-too-familiar sound of ice popping and cracking. Except this time, it wasn't somewhere off in the distance. It was really close. In fact, it was coming from the same bus-sized block of ice we were standing on.

Sherpas believe in reincarnation and generally aren't afraid of dying. If they've lived a good life, they come back as a higher being and have an even better life, constantly moving up the celestial ladder, so to speak. Therefore they aren't necessarily afraid of anything. At least that's what I was told, so when I noticed a little nervousness from Kame, I immediately knew that something wasn't right.

I started getting nervous because he seemed nervous, which fed into him getting more nervous, which made me even more nervous . . .

All of a sudden Kame started chanting. "Om mani padme hum," while rocking back and forth.

"Our Father who art in Heaven . . ." I prayed aloud, as the lady continued her ridiculously slow descent on the ladder. By this point I'm starting to freak out. "Hey! Lady!" I shouted. "You gotta move—we're coming down!"

Kame mounted the ladder first and began his way down. I was right on his tail. When we both safely reached the little platform on the ice below, we watched in shock as everything we had just been standing on collapsed and disappeared into a dark crevasse. We had nearly died.

Things like this happen all the time in the Khumbu Icefall. It's constantly moving and settling, just like that glass of ice, only on a more massive scale. We were a few of the lucky ones.

When you want to do something no one has ever done before, you understand the risks involved, and you have to be willing to take those risks. You have to be willing to face your fears when you really want something, and I wanted this more than anything.

My body was prepared for the altitude. My mind was ready for the push to the summit. I crawled into my tent for one of the last night's sleeps before moving up the mountain to the pre-established camps for a potential summit attempt. Throughout the acclimatization period I had returned to Base Camp every night, where I would either read or write while lying on my corrugated foam sleeping pad. That pad was always with me on the mountain, giving me comfort and warmth to rest and sleep on the icy surface beneath. Every night I'd lay on it as I wrote my goals and affirmations and then read them out loud to myself. The first time I took it camping in Colorado, I took a Sharpie and wrote "Everest – 29,035" at the top. It was just like those sticky notes on the side of the mirror, and it served as a constant reminder of my goal, a way to keep me focused.

During my time on Everest, I'd written other words on those corrugated slats, things like, "You can do this," or "You will make history," or "The higher I go, the stronger I get." That last one was the most important to me, and I'd repeat them with nearly every step I took climbing the mountain. With one step, I would say, "The higher I go," and with the next, "the stronger I get." If I could get my brain to believe it, I knew it would come true.

I also visualized my bone marrow as a factory, and inside the factory there was a conveyor belt. That might sound odd, but it worked. Inside my bone marrow, I pictured this conveyor belt as the main component of the blood factory. At the beginning of the belt, I pictured a machine that laid down a cell wall. That cell wall then moved down the conveyor belt where the next machine would bend it into a "U" shape. After the U-shaped cell wall was formed, it was moved to the next station where it was filled with plasma. Continuing on down the belt, it was filled with mitochondria, a cell nucleus, and everything it needed to form a new red blood cell. At the end, it was pinched closed and soldered shut, then blasted out into my body as a new cell. This was just another tool I used to motivate myself and help my body manufacture more red blood cells and hemoglobin. I wanted every possible opportunity to be successful and, therefore, I was pulling out all the stops.

The night before I was going to leave Base Camp and push to the summit, I lay down on my pad and flipped over onto my stomach to read the affirmations and positive notes. Everest. You can do this. You are strong. You can do anything you put your mind to. Cancer didn't stop you, Everest won't either. Everest is just a hill—this is going to be great! Enjoy every moment.

I was careful to not put anything negative like, "Don't fall" or "Don't fail." That would be telling me to not do something. It's like putting a kid into a room with a button that says "DO NOT PUSH." What do you think is going to happen? It's the same thing with adults. If you're walking down the street and you keep telling yourself, "Don't trip, don't trip," what's going to happen? You're going to trip, that's what. Instead, it's better to say something positive like, "Walk tall, be strong, have firm footing." If you think positively, your brain will make it happen. I know from experience. It's all positive, all the time. And Everest was no different.

After reading every one of the affirmations, I flipped over onto my back and once again began to visualize myself on the summit. Closing my eyes, I went through the routine that had become like second nature. A slow, deep, and full breath in through my nose while tensing every muscle. A pause while I held my breath, then a long, slow exhale through my mouth, letting my muscles relax again. I did this over and over until I was on the verge of falling asleep. I pictured myself taking the last few steps to the summit, feeling the warmth of the sun to my right, the wind on my body. I could smell the cold, feel the goggles and oxygen mask on my face. I could also hear the whispers of all the millions and millions of people who've ever been touched by cancer, beckoning me to the summit, encouraging me to push forward and remain strong. As I drifted off to sleep, a smile on my face, I was already at the top.

I was already successful.

Chapter 10

I woke up early to the sound of Kame tapping the tent. It had been a sound, restful sleep (no bizarre dreams about M&Ms or Disney World). The sun wasn't even up yet, but I knew we had to get through the Khumbu Icefall before that big heater in the sky started warming up the ice. That's when things start to shuffle, slide around, and collapse. At night, everything re-freezes, and becomes more stable again. So it's safest to climb and get through the icefall as early as possible. I had already done it many times, so I was ready for it.

Breakfast with Seth was quieter than normal. It was surreal, actually. We both knew this would be the last time I'd leave Base Camp as I pushed for the summit. And, more sobering, we understood that if things didn't go well, this could be last time we'd ever see each other.

"How you feeling?" Seth asked.

"I'm okay." My short response revealed my nervousness.

"Sounds like it," he said sarcastically. Then he got more serious. "Look, you can do this. You've put in the work, you've put in the time, your body is ready. The only thing that would possibly hold you back is the weather."

I nodded. "Yeah, and it looks clear on the fifteenth, so we're hoping to leave Camp Three the day before and head up. You'll be my eyes and ears after that. If you tell me to turn around, I'll turn around." I paused and then looked my brother in the eyes. "You're an integral part of this, you know. You always were. I wouldn't be here if it wasn't for you."

Seth smiled. "I know. And I'll be honest with you, too. I want you to listen to me. You might not be thinking clearly up there."

"You're my brother, and I'm going to do everything I can to make it, but if you say I need to turn around, that's what I'll do. You're the one who's going to be thinking clearly. Just don't tell me to walk off the side of the mountain."

"Hey, I can't make any promises," he joked. "Don't worry, I'll make sure you do the right things up there."

Up in what's called the Death Zone (above 26,000 feet), often times climbers can't think straight because their brains are starved for oxygen. As a result, they make poor decisions— decisions that, in many cases, have resulted in death.

Like my parents had said before I left, I didn't fight through two cancers just to die on some hunk of rock and ice. I knew I was in good hands with Seth. Sure, we had the typical sibling rivalry when we were younger, but that was all in the past. This was serious business, and I knew Seth was going to make the right decisions for me.

Heading up to my camp's stupa (a temporary structure built where our prayer flags flew over camp), we lit sage—a traditional Buddhist offering for protection—and I quickly said a prayer. This was it. This was what I'd been training so hard for over the past eight months. In my mind I had seen it happen countless times. But this time it was real. I was about to take on one of the most difficult challenges on the face of the Earth.

Every time we would hike through Base Camp to get to the base of the Khumbu Icefall, the Sherpas and I would joke around, toss rocks at each other's feet and trip one another. This time was different. No one spoke a word. I kept picturing myself on the top of the mountain, imagining the conveyor belt of blood cells working overtime.

At the edge of the icefall, we all sat down on our packs and started putting on our crampons. For the first time real self-doubt creeped into my mind.

Are you ready for this? Can you do this? Do you think you've trained enough? What about your gear? What if it fails? What if you're on the fixed ropes and they break free from the ice? What if a whole column of climbers above you falls and tumbles, taking you with them? What if . . . STOP! This isn't helping.

I glanced up at Kame and Ang Dorgee, who just happened to be looking at me at the same time. Both with a peculiar look on their faces. "AAAAHHHH!" I screamed, in order to break the ice, so to speak. Then we all erupted into laughter, easing the incredible tension of the moment. After that, all the negative talk in my head drifted away, and I felt more like myself again. Everyone has self-doubt from time to time, but this was neither the time nor the place for negativity.

So, with our crampons strapped to our boots, our packs on our backs, and ice axes in hand, we headed up into the Khumbu Icefall. I took one last look back at Seth and the group, who had followed us to the base of the icefall, before we rounded a huge serac (chunk of ice) and lost sight of them.

Climbing up and over the "icescrapers," we made our way across a few ladders, one of which I had slipped on the first time I had crossed it and nearly plummeted to my death. By this time, however, I had already navigated across it well over a dozen times, and I walked over it with confidence, continually telling myself, "The higher I go, the stronger I get."

We continued to move forward one step at a time, navigating through the minefield of crevasses and ever-unstable ice flow. Cresting the top of the ridge, the sun was waiting for us as we caught up to another group. When their Sherpa saw me climbing and keeping up with Kame and Ang Dorgee, he started laughing. He told me I was an incredibly strong climber and called me a Sherpa. Eventually I earned the name "Dawa Dorgee" because I was such a strong climber compared to other "clients" they had worked with. I think they respected me because I never treated them like servants, but rather as friends and partners in my quest, which for them is definitely not the norm. But come to think of it, normal's never been my thing.

We stopped at Camp One briefly to rest and adjust to the altitude and then continued into the Western Cwm (pronounced coom), where temperatures could reach up to eighty degrees or drop into negative digits, depending upon the wind. This day, luckily, there was only a light wind, and the sun was bright and warm. We all felt amazing as we continued to the final and most dangerous ladder crossing on our climb.

Spanning the largest and deepest crevasse on the route, this expansive crossing consisted of five aluminum ladders tied together—five!—with pickets and ice screws attached to the sides of the ladder on both sides of the crevasse. Attached to these pickets, which are basically temporary anchors designed to stop a climber (in theory) from tumbling into the bottomless pit, were thin ropes or cord that help with balance while you're making your way across.

Ang Dorgee went first. I leaned over and grabbed the cord on each side of the ladder, leaning backwards and pulling on the other ends to make them taut. Slowly he made his way safely to the other side, then kept his hands on the cords and leaning forward to make the ropes taut for me. By this point I had made this crossing at least fifteen times, but that didn't make it any easier. Every time I'd get to the middle, the ladder would bow, reminding me that these sections were tied together. I tried to keep my eyes on the rungs as I crossed, but I couldn't help but notice the gaping, seemingly bottomless black hole beneath me.

As I reached the other side, I let out a huge sigh of relief, which made Ang Dorgee chuckle (remember, they're not afraid of dying). I then leaned forward to make the cord taut and help Kame as he too made his way across.

With the ladder behind us, we slowly made our way up to Camp Two where we were to spend the next couple of nights resting and keeping an eye on the weather. This was also the same location where a few weeks earlier I had experienced my first infamous Everest storm.

Back home in Colorado, I loved storms, as long as I was indoors, that is. But up here, where my only protection was the micron-thick fabric of my tent, it was a different story altogether. During that earlier storm, hurricane-force winds had pummeled our tent for two days and two nights straight. I hardly got any sleep at all as I tried to hold up the frame of my tent, praying that it wouldn't rip apart. I actually lost my friend Peter during that storm. He was up at Camp Three and couldn't find his own tent, so he just jumped into someone else's unoccupied tent, but he didn't have any food or water for the duration of the storm. Delirious on his way down, he mis-clipped on a guide rope and tumbled over 2000 feet into a crevasse and died.

As we rested at Camp Two, we were relieved to hear that the weather looked great for a summit bid on the fifteenth of May. A couple of days later we pushed onward and upward to Camp Three, with plans to move on to Camp Four the next day, and then hopefully the summit the day after.

Unpacking at Camp Three on the side of the Lhotse Face, we tethered ourselves into the ice screws so we wouldn't rocket down the mile-long, forty-five-degree sheet of ice. (This is where my friend had died.) As I was sitting there getting ready to melt snow for water and boil some for our freeze-dried dinner, I felt odd. I couldn't put my finger on it, but something didn't feel right. I just brushed it off and figured it was exhaustion, nothing a good night's sleep wouldn't fix.

Later that evening, Seth and I were back on the walkie-talkies again. Back at Base Camp, he had been updating the website about my adventure, and he wanted to know what he should send out to the world regarding my progress. He was also writing about the issues we were having on the mountain, things you'd never even think about, but that would easily prevent a successful summit if we didn't get things dialed in. The solar panels needed to be working properly in order to charge the car batteries that we used for power. Of course, he first had to find them, and when he did, he had to find the acid to put into the batteries in order for them to hold a charge. Little things, but important.

These issues, however, didn't seem so important at the moment, with his older brother miles away, stuck in a tent at around 23,000 feet and unable to even walk.

Seth's voice trembled while he spoke. "So . . . what do you want me to write about today?"

"I'm thinking," I replied, knowing these could be the last words I ever shared with the world.

A few minutes went by before my brother radioed back. "You there?"

"Okay," I said, "you can tell them that I left Camp Two at about eight in the morning, and about an hour from Camp Three, Sean felt like crap."

"Or maybe a more PC term?"

"How about cow dung?"

"Or better yet, yak dung. We are in Nepal, after all."

"Fine. And then he began to think about climbing this stupid mountain and the reasons why he's here...and those are the only reasons that kept him going." I managed to get those words past my lips just as my voice started to crack. Then the fear set in. "He should have turned around," I continued, tears welling up inside me. The thin air came into my lung in short, small spurts while I trembled, trying to choke back the tears. Who was I trying to fool? I was doing my best to hold it together, but everyone back at Base Camp could hear how nervous I was, how scared I sounded. I had to pull myself together. I had to be the strong person that everyone was depending on.

"Okay." Seth's voice came across the radio, breaking the silence and bringing me back to the moment. "Go ahead."

I continued talking into the walkie-talkie. "He got to Camp Three, the furthest tent away from, uhhhh . . . Camp Two, of course, and yacked green bile. Thought that maybe he should go back down. Now he's lying in a hot, festering tent, waiting for the sun to go down so he can get some cold water." At such extreme altitudes, when the sun is out there's not much atmosphere to filter out its intense radiation, so it's actually excruciatingly hot. I was in desperate need of some cold water to lower my body's temperature and get it back to normal.

"How about you drink some hot water first," Seth suggested. When the air is this dry, it's easy for the throat to be parched simply by breathing. Hot or warm water is easier for the body to digest and actually helps with this problem.

Knowing I couldn't talk much longer without completely losing my composure and blubbering like a fool, I signed off. "I'm going to hook up the oxygen bottle and see what it feels like." I grabbed the mask connected to the orange oxygen bottle, pulled the rubber straps over my head, and drew in a deep breath of the richness my body so needed. In the distance, the sun was quickly dipping below the mountains, and I attempted to choke down a little dehydrated stew. The cubed carrots didn't look any better than the wilted green peas or the flaccid, no-longer-spiral noodles within the mixture of what looked like the insides of someone else's stomach that had been thrown up into my bowl.

I hydrated and tried to keep the food down while still breathing in the flowing oxygen. I closed my eyes and began my visualization again, trying to get myself back, and fell asleep.

Eventually, I drifted off to sleep, praying again for yet another miracle.

I woke up violently ill. In extreme altitudes the human body goes into protection mode in order to save the vital organs. Blood actually recedes from appendages and collects around the liver, lungs, and heart. I had never experienced anything like this before. My fingers were tingly. My stomach was upset. My toes were numb. I felt a wave of nausea come over me like I hadn't felt since my last chemo treatment. I knew what was coming next, so I unzipped the tent as quickly as I could and vomited.

I felt dizzy, fuzzy-headed, almost like I was intoxicated. I radioed down to Seth to check in and let him know what was happening. There were no secrets up here. You have to be honest about everything, otherwise someone (me, in particular) could die.

"Hey, Sean," he said. "How'd it go last night?"

I mumbled something incoherently, to which Seth simply replied, "Huh?"

I laughed and told him that I saw my dinner again this morning, that I felt like I'd gotten hit by a bus, and that I couldn't think or move too well.

After a lengthy discussion, we decided I should do a field-sobriety-like test (i.e., heel toe, heel toe) in order to gauge my coordination. On Lhotse Face it's incredibly difficult to find any piece of land on which to do this type of walking test, but I was able to find a suitable spot right next to my tent. It took me about ten minutes of huffing and puffing to put on each boot. My muscles just couldn't get enough oxygen to sustain the effort I was asking of them. When I finally got them on, I stood up, nearly wobbling off the mountain in the process. I was determined to do this exercise, which would give us a good idea how well I was handling the altitude. After just one step, I knew my brain wasn't functioning anywhere near full capacity. With my left foot planted, I tried to put the heel of my right foot on the toes of the other. But it instead it ended up on the other side of the straight line, nowhere near my left toes. I tried the same thing with the opposite foot and got similar results. After multiple attempts, I simply couldn't do it. I couldn't walk straight—a slight problem when you're trying to climb the world's highest mountain.

I got back into the tent and radioed Seth. "Sean to Base Camp. Seth, do you copy?"

"Yo!"

"Sorry it took so long," I said. "Up here everything takes a hundred times longer than you'd think. It's crazy."

"No problem. How'd it go?"

I hesitated. "You want the truth?"

"At this point, anything but the truth would be detrimental, and potentially deadly."

"I couldn't do it."

Long silence.

"I couldn't put one foot in front of the other. Not to save my life."

After a long conversation about my options, we decided it would be best for me to hook up my mask and sleep on oxygen that night.

I had just spent nearly a month and a half on ice-covered Everest, climbing up and down countless times in order to establish different camps and get my body used to the extreme altitude. During this acclimatization period, my body had been manufacturing more red blood cells and hemoglobin in order to be more efficient in this altitude. But something was wrong. Terribly wrong. As I lay in my tent at about 23,000 feet, wrapped up in my negative-forty-degree sleeping bag, my brain was swelling. Just outside my makeshift shelter, I was tethered to some pickets hammered into the bulletproof ice. These were the only things holding me to the side of the mountain. Below stretched an expansive, forty-five-degree-steep glacier that fell for nearly a mile. I couldn't even think without getting dizzy and suffering extreme anxiety and vertigo.

I knew I was dying . . . again.

Over the course of the past year, I had pushed my body to its limit, constantly breaking it down, only to build it back up, stronger and better. I had pushed out whatever self-doubt tried to infiltrate my mind, focusing on the positive and visualizing myself on the summit. One way or another, I knew I was going to make it.

But this was different. This was completely unexpected. This was horrible. This was deadly. I was on the side of the highest mountain on Earth with a swelling brain. Had all the training been worthless? What was going to happen? How was I going to survive this? I was plagued with self-doubt as I lay inside my tent, oxygen mask strapped to my face. Breathing deeply, I remembered that the only cure for HACE was to retreat to a lower altitude. I couldn't allow that to happen. Not now. Not when I was so close.

That night it seemed like I woke up every five minutes. I was in and out of consciousness trying to figure out what was going on. I started thinking about everything I had gone through in my life. Cancer. The horrible treatments. Remission. Cancer again. More horrible treatments. Nearly dying (many times over). Losing an entire year of my life. Going into remission again. Getting back in the pool and working so hard to win the championship. High school. College. Grad school. Struggling with what to do with my life. Deciding to climb Everest. Moving to Colorado. Being homeless for more than a month. The months of hard training. Being rejected again and again before finally finding a sponsor. Traveling around the world to Nepal. Spending over a month getting my mind and body used to the altitude and ready for the push to the summit.

And now, here I was . . . so close to the summit . . . so close to reaching my goal . . . so close to dying.

I laid there the entire day and night, fighting for my life. If it had been the first time I'd ever been in this position, I might have given up. But it wasn't the first or even the second time. I had been here before, on the brink of death, and I had fought and fought and given everything I had until I didn't think I could give any more. I didn't understand it then. Why I had to go through it all, all that pain, all that fear, all that doubt, but now, suddenly, it all made sense. Everything I had gone through when I was young and battling cancer had hardened me and prepared me to face whatever life threw in front of me. All that pain, all that sickness, losing my hair, losing a year of my life . . . it had all been my mental training ground for this latest battle, this latest fight for my life. But my mind was too strong to allow this latest challenge, this latest roadblock stop me from my end goal. After all, in my mind, I had already been to the top, hundreds of times over. It was already real to me, and nothing was going to stop me, not even my own swelling brain, from reaching my goal, from making it to the top of the world!

I can't explain what happened next. No one can. No one recovers from HACE without going back down the mountain to a lower altitude. It was the only way to relieve the pressure on the brain and stop it from swelling. Yet, by that second day, the pressure had gone down, the swelling had subsided, and once again I was feeling like myself. I was ready to complete what I had come all this way to finish.

Those two nights and the day between seemed like forever, but it turned out to be a blessing in disguise. All the others who were on the same schedule as me to make a bid for the summit on the fifteenth had left Camp Three when I couldn't move. They had made it up to Camp Four, but then, the weather turned bad, and they were forced to turn back, losing their only chance of reaching the summit that season. Had I not fallen ill and had I actually gone with everyone else to Camp Four, I too would have missed my opportunity to reach the top. It was like it was meant to be.

After those couple days resting and sleeping on the oxygen, I felt 100 percent better and ready to make my attempt at history.

Crawling out of my tent, I could see the vast, snow-covered glacial valley stretched out before me. The sun reflected off the cold whiteness, reminding me of the reasons I was on the side of Mt. Everest. Everyone on Earth who's ever been touched by cancer was there in spirit, pulling me along and helping me up the world's highest peak. I could sense their struggles and hardships. I could feel their pain, agony, and despair. I could hear their many voices whispering words of encouragement. From deep within my heart, I could hear them calling out to me: "Sean! You can do this!"

After plodding up to Camp Four at over 26,000 feet, I radioed down to Seth to tell him we were safe at the South Col and were going to prepare for a summit push later that night around 8:00 p.m.

Sometime later I had fallen asleep, and when I slowly began to wake up, I glanced down at my watch, thinking I had maybe been out for five minutes or so. I was shocked to see it was 10:30 p.m. I bolted up and looked over at Kame and Ang Dorgee, who were just as shocked—we had slept through our alarm clocks! How could this have happened? As quickly as possible, we got ready to head out into the dark, frozen night and head up the mountain with our headlamps.

I picked up the radio. "Sean to Base Camp. Seth, do you copy?"

"Hey!" came Seth's reply. "We've been trying to reach you. What's going on?"

"Dude, I don't know. We slept through our alarm clocks. Every other group is on the mountain, and we're two hours behind them. We better get going. I'll radio more from the mountain."

"Okay, be safe. We'll keep the fire going." The Sherpas believe it's good luck to keep the fire at Base Camp burning with sage. And since I needed all the luck I could get, Seth kept the fire going throughout the entire night while I was making my attempt at the summit.

I emerged from the tent at the last camp and peered up at all the climbers ahead of us. It looked like a string of Christmas lights with one head lamp after another shining in the frigid, dark night. Our goal was to summit by ten the next morning. That was our turnaround time. No matter how close we were at that point, we would have to turn around.

The mountain was eerily quiet as we made our way from the relatively flat surface of the South Col toward the steep incline of the last 3000 vertical feet to the summit. With my headlamp lighting the way and every bit of skin covered—including my three-inch thick mittens, which kept my fingers from freezing and falling off—I began moving toward the ultimate goal I had been picturing in my mind for so long. Step by step, inch by inch, I made my way in the dark, windless night up the ever-steeper section of the mountain.

Eventually we caught the caboose of the train of people I had seen from back at Camp Four hours before. Time meant nothing to me. My stomach was in my throat, my heart was pounding in my ears, and I couldn't feel anything from my knees down. It was so cold, so unfathomably cold. The night seemed to go on forever. All along, the one thing that kept me company was a tiny digital media player in my left hand. I had strung the cord under my clothes up my arm, and inserted only one ear bud so I could hear the outside world. Honestly, I wanted to be able to hear if there were any falling bodies. I didn't want to become part of a human avalanche.

As I looked at the climbers ahead of me, I could tell by the light of their headlamps on the snow ahead of them that they had stopped moving. Dozens of lights sat unmoving, frozen. Except for mine, which was dancing on the snow as my head bobbed to the sound of my music. I was determined to enjoy every second of this historic moment, and the music gave me the energy I needed to push on.

I bounced on my feet to keep the blood flowing and curled my toes in my boots to, hopefully, keep them from getting frostbitten. The human body is about 65 percent water, and your blood is pushing 90 percent. When water freezes, it expands. When the water inside human cells freezes—which is what frostbite is—it expands and causes swelling. Eventually the cell wall is pushed to its limit and breaks. When it thaws, the tissue is dead. I had seen this happen to another climber a few days earlier on the Lhotse Iceface. The thumb on his right hand was frozen black, and it looked like a mushroom. I was praying that the same thing wouldn't happen to my toes. Meanwhile I kept bouncing up and down, curling my toes, and doing my best to keep focusing on the summit.

Just as I thought it couldn't possibly get any colder, we were hit by a fifty-mph gust of wind that nearly knocked me off balance and into the abyss to my right. Another one followed, and I dug my ice ax into the snow, hoping it would keep me anchored to the mountainside. The merciless wind smacked me in the face, scoffing at my goggles, down hood, wool stocking cap, and oxygen mask. I thought for sure my cheeks and eyeballs would be frozen solid. I braced myself for another icy blast, but it never came. Chomolungma had taken her best shots at knocking me off her peak and failed. Now it was almost as if she was welcoming me to continue on. The rest of the night was one of the calmest I'd ever experienced on a mountain.

After catching the train of people, Kame and Ang Dorgee suggested we unhook from the fixed rope and continue upwards on our own. The others were going too slowly to be successful. We had to keep moving. Unhooking from the safety rope was both frightening and exhilarating. On Everest, if you're advancing at roughly five feet per *minute*, you're moving incredibly quickly. Yet here I was, with half the normal person's lung capacity, moving at around ten feet per minute and making amazing progress. After passing the lower column of climbers, we made our way back to the fixed rope to continue forward until we caught the next car on the train of climbers. Again, we unclipped, went around that group, and made our way back to the relative safety of the guide rope.

By this time it must have been around 6:00 a.m., because off in the distance I could see the first rays of the sun inching up over the horizon. I looked to my right, and it literally dropped two miles down into Tibet. One little misstep and I would tumble to my death. To my left it dropped off as well, but it was only about one and half miles to the bottom. When you reach this part of the summit push, they say if you want to live longer, make sure you fall off the right side. You have an extra half mile to fall. Climbers sure have a warped sense of humor.

I had never seen anything more spectacular, and I couldn't imagine anything more beautiful. The clouds stretched out like an ocean; the mountain peaks were little islands scattered out as far as the eye could see. And up this high, that's pretty far. Out along the horizon was the most incredible, most amazing sunrise I had ever seen. The most intense purples, yellows, oranges, blues, and pinks—it was absolutely stunning. And then it hit me. As I looked a little closer, I could see that the horizon wasn't flat. Up this high, at the very top of the world, the horizon is curved. I could actually see the curvature of the Earth. *This can't be any better, I thought. This couldn't possibly be more amazing.*

But then it was. As I turned and looked off to my left, it was still dark. There, straight out ahead of me…stars. I was looking at stars at eye level! I stood there smiling and in awe, choking back the tears. I knew right then that I was where I was meant be at that moment in time. This was my moment. I was going to make it to the top.

All the visualization I had done over the past year made the rest of the climb to the summit almost like deja vu. The crunching of the snow under my feet I had heard hundreds of times before. The wind a gentle breeze on my face. The white snow so pristine. The horizon so spectacular. This was it. I had been here before. I was home.

When I finally reached the summit that morning, I collapsed to my knees, pulled off my oxygen mask, and there was that smell—the smell of ozone, just as I had imagined it. It was true. It was real. *This* was real.

I was on top of the world.

My head in my hands and weeping like an infant, I radioed down to my brother, who had been up all night feeding sage to the fire by the stupa. "I did it, Seth! I made it to the top! We did it . . . together!"

Seth got on the satellite phone and called home, where it was 11:47 p.m. in South Carolina. Mom answered, with Dad right there next to her, and Seth said, "Right now, at this moment in time, you have a son who's standing on top of the world!"

It was an incredible moment, and we were all so emotional. But, of course, I had a higher purpose for being there.

I pulled out a silk flag that I had carried with me in my chest pocket, right next to my heart. On it I had written "Dedicated to all those affected by cancer in this small world!! Keep Climbing!!" Along with the names of so many people who had been touched by cancer—those who'd fought and survived, those who were still fighting the good fight, and those who had fought so hard but lost the battle. They had been my hope, my inspiration. Whenever I had felt exhausted, and like I couldn't take another step, they were the ones who had carried me all the way to the top.

I took that flag and wrapped it around the summit as an homage to everyone who's ever been touched by cancer, to serve as a beacon of hope for all. I could hear their voices now, all congratulating me on this accomplishment, for taking on this historic challenge and achieving my goal.

But of course, I knew this was just the beginning. Sitting on top of the world, my climb had just begun.

Part III
Begin Your Own
Success Journey

By Lance Snow

Chapter 11

Our thoughts then direct our actions,
and those actions shape our lives.
—Sean Swarner

"**E**verest—a name synonymous with majesty, mystery, and greatness...but also with misery and death."

Does this statement about the world's highest mountain also describe the same feelings about achieving your own dream? Does it feel like a daunting task requiring Herculean effort? Does it seem more than just out of reach?

You just went on an amazing journey with Sean. He shared with you stories of his childhood growing up in Willard, Ohio. You learned how he overcame two different cancers. He shared his decision to climb Mt. Everest and how he trained for this amazing feat. And, finally he took you on the adventure of a lifetime up Mt. Everest to honor everyone on Earth who has been touched by cancer. During these stories a theme emerged. Sean visualized and saw his success before he even began.

In this section, we will spend some time on the first step of your own success journey. This will be your first summit of success. You will:

- Define your dream.
- Visualize your dream.
- Create new habits to begin to move toward your dream on your own success journey.

It is fitting that Mt. Everest was the first of the Seven Summits Sean climbed. Mt. Everest is the tallest mountain in the world making it possibly the biggest challenge in the pursuit of the Seven Summits. Just like Everest, this step in achieving your dream may be the biggest mountain to climb. For some it may be fairly simple; for others, this may be the most challenging part of their success journey.

Defining Your Dream

In his story, Sean started by visualizing what his personal dream was before he even began. He fully and completely believed it was real. In battling his cancers, he imagined himself in remission; he imagined he was his cancer-fighting alter-ego, Interplanetary Body Captain Spaceman Spiff defending his body and attacking the cancer and did so with finite detail. As he prepared for Mt. Everest, he saw himself already on the summit, which not only helped him prepare and train, but it helped him get through so many challenges on his journey both big and small. He used visualization to make his dream his reality and we'll use that to make your dream a reality.

Before we can visualize anything, we must begin by defining your dream. You need to be as clear and as detailed as possible and fill in the blanks with your imagination. You will also need to spend some time putting meaning behind your dream.

Imagine for a moment that Sean wasn't clear about standing on the top of Mt. Everest. What if Sean maybe kind of sort of wanted to try to climb a mountain? Maybe any mountain? And, what if he sort of knew there was some kind of meaning behind it? Maybe he never took the time to discover what it was or maybe he didn't even consider it at all? Do you think he would have been successful? Sure he probably would have spent time, energy, and resources just trying to find a way to climb some mountain. He might have taken some climbing classes. It's possible that he could have even climbed a significant mountain. If he wasn't clear, he could have backed away from an amazing life changing idea. Without a clearly defined dream with significant meaning behind it, there could have been many things that kept him from even starting, let alone actually climbing Mt. Everest.

When you are on any journey, be it climbing a mountain or pursuing a dream, there will be barriers that will stand in your way. Before you begin to define your dream, let's discuss some common barriers most people face when starting their success journey. It's important we address them before clearly defining your dream, because many of these barriers will affect how big or meaningful this dream of yours is. You need to define your dream as if these barriers do not exist; so it's best to address them before you even begin and acknowledge that some of them may confront you on every step of your success journey.

Chapter 12
Overcoming the Barriers
to Success

Sean shared with us the many challenges that he faced on his quest to climb Mt. Everest. Some of these challenges were somewhat easy to overcome because he uncovered the problems early. Cerebral edema, however, was a life-threatening challenge that needed careful consideration. Any one of these problems could have caused Sean to pack up his bags and head for home if he had not already defined his dream and visualized himself already standing on the summit of Mt. Everest.

One way to eliminate some of the barriers you will face on your success journey is by addressing some of them up front. Before embarking on any expedition, or personal endeavor, you must first get in the right mindset before you can begin to define what your dream looks like.

Let's discuss some of the barriers you might come across before your personal journey even begins, before you even begin to define your dream. Some of these barriers may be obvious to you. Some barriers may be surprises. But any one of these may cause you to short change yourself when defining your dream and ultimately force you to create a dream that isn't really yours.

Barrier 1: Negative Self Talk

Am I really good enough? I don't have . . . experience, knowledge skills, intelligence, etc.

This barrier could be as big as the mountain itself. Too many people have convinced themselves that they can't achieve their dreams and they don't even know it. This is probably the greatest barrier for any of us. We tune in to what others say to us and say about us. We spend too much time deliberating and considering what others think about us. And, yes, we need to ignore those people and let it go, but that isn't what this section is about. The truth is we don't spend nearly enough time listening to what we say to ourselves. We need to tune into to our own thoughts and understand how they relate to our self-concept.

Have you ever heard a catchy song, and it repeats in your head over and over? Some have called that an "ear bug." It gets stuck in your mind and you often find yourself automatically singing it or humming it out loud. Self-talk happens in a similar way. We get what we think about ourselves stuck in our heads and then repeat. It blends in and we find ourselves automatically acting in the way that is consistent with those self-talk messages.

Imagine being exposed to the same recorded messages over and over again. After a while, if you haven't been driven mad by it, it will begin to become background. You might think that is a good thing but this just means we have begun to accept it, regardless of what it is saying. It becomes the background of our thoughts.

Stop and take a moment to think about this for a while: what are you saying or thinking about yourself? Are you thinking positive or negative thoughts about yourself? If you keep telling yourself you aren't good at math, guess what? You have given up all hope that you will become good at math. If you are telling yourself all the time that you are a "clutterbug" and disorganized, then guess what? You will just accept the fact that you will never be orderly and organized. If you keep telling yourself that your artwork or movie scripts or designs or whatever it is isn't good enough, then you have talked yourself into never moving forward with your creations. You have already convinced yourself that you will come up short. In your mind you are already asking yourself, "Why bother?" Take a moment and consider whether you do this or not. What are your examples?

What if instead we begin to reprogram what we say to ourselves? What might that look like?

What do you think Sean was telling himself during each step of his journey to the summit of Mt. Everest? I'm sure if there were thoughts of "what are you doing?" that followed with the conscious thoughts of "I am doing this; I will reach the summit. I have come this far; I will continue forward and upward. I am doing this for everyone touched by cancer, I will make them proud."

Consider this analogy that Sean uses in his speeches:

"Your thoughts are like water. The glass of water is like your brain. Negative thoughts are dirty water. Positive thoughts are clear water. If your head is filled with negative thoughts then your brain is essentially a glass of dirty water. What happens if you have a glass of dirty water and put it under a stream of clean water from the faucet? Eventually, it becomes clear water, or positive thoughts. You flush out the dirty water, or negative thoughts, and are left with positive thoughts."

Rinse your brain of the negative thoughts. We start simply by listening. Listening to yourself is how you begin to change your self-monologue and become a more positive thinker. It is that simple. And, that is also why it is so hard. It is hard to maintain that conscious awareness of your thoughts and essentially police them to change them when necessary.

Awareness – Listen and become aware. You will be surprised what thoughts you have about yourself. Do not get upset from what you hear as we all are prone to it. You first just need to be aware.

Interrupt – Stop your negative self-talk when you recognize it. I used to wear a rubber band on my wrist and snap it when I would catch myself thinking negatively about myself. At times that was a painful way to shift my thinking but it worked.

Replace – Some people pick a word like "stop" or "erase" and then consciously replace the negative talk with positive affirming talk. An example of replacing negative with positive is: When you're walking, and your inner voice is telling you, "don't trip," replace it with, "stand tall, walk strong."

The positive and affirming talk is often the opposite of what you were negatively telling yourself. To be even more purposeful with this activity, you can pre-choose some statements such as "I am excellent at . . ." or "I am successful at . . ." to help make the positive statements more automatic.

Make It Daily – As you are reviewing your dream statement and visualizing, add a moment of proactive daily affirmation. Repeat some positive statements about yourself over and over during a predetermined time during your day. If you are able to look at yourself in the mirror, that is even better as you will be face to face with yourself and truly see yourself say these things.

Reflect – Finally, add some reflective time to personally acknowledge things you have done well each day. If you had a particularly rough day, you can always acknowledge past achievements that you are proud of and use those.

These steps are an ongoing part of your success journey. Just like some types of exercises or new skills, it may take a while to build your "positive self-talk" muscles; but once you do and create the habit, they are but momentary positive reflections that help protect you from the negative self-talk that looks to sabotage your success journey.

Barrier 2: Dream Guilt

How can I chase and achieve my dream when there are so many people out there . . . suffering, starving, in poverty, struggling, etc.?

This is certainly a real dilemma that many people struggle with. They feel they cannot chase their dreams and have success because there are so many people that won't chase their dreams or even can't chase their dream.

There could be many reasons why someone may feel guilty about their dream:

Poverty – Consider the person who grew up with modest means or had a rather difficult childhood. Maybe they still have close ties to people or a place that doesn't typically foster the type of dream they are dreaming. This person may feel guilty about pursuing their dream because their roots are buried deep in the lifestyle in which they were raised. They feel a connection to the people or way of life and they may feel that they are abandoning their roots. In reality, chasing and achieving their dream may allow them to create opportunities for others allowing them to give back; or even better…inspire others to chase their own dreams!

Illness – How about the person who has a sick family member or friend and they simply feel bad that this person has to endure an illness. As a result, they hold back chasing their dream out of fear of making this person feel bad because they can't pursue their own dreams at the moment. In reality, maybe the person with this illness will serve as motivation for them to chase their dream. Maybe these actions will even inspire the person with the illness. When Sean was summiting Everest, he had the collective will of all of those who were affected by cancer helping him to the top.

Your Illness – What about the person who is currently ill in some way, shape, or form? Certainly there are circumstances where you must focus on your health first and foremost, but, why not make that the dream or at least the first step in a long-term dream. When Sean was battling the separate cancers, his main dream was to be healthy again and regain a normal childhood.

Religion – In many religions, some are taught that greed is a sin and they may even see their dream or the products of their dream as greedy. We should be giving away our worldly goods and material items to others who are wanting, right? Yes, that is true to an extent; but we are given skills, talents, and deep desires that need to be manifested. In reality, by chasing our dream and succeeding, we will be able to give back so much more in return.

Others – Finally, how about all of those people that you interact with on a daily basis who don't seem to be acting on their dreams? I am talking about family, friends, co-workers, etc. who move through life with a cynical eye for anything out of the "normal." Are you holding back on your dream for fear that they will condemn you? Or are you holding back because you are afraid of making them feel bad because they aren't chasing their dream and you are? In reality, these are precisely the people who need to see you chase your dream and succeed. For whatever reason, they can't see themselves chasing their dream or they may not even be aware they have a dream to chase or even that it is okay to chase the dream. They need that person in their life to show them it can happen for them too. Show them it can be done!

The reality behind all of these possible reasons is that you should be conscious of those around you. We should be aware there are people who are ill or are struggling and need some help. We need to give to others and help them where and when we can. Giving is at the core of what achieving your dream is all about. After all, when you write your dream statement you are identifying the meaning behind what you are doing.

The world needs what you have to offer. You have your dream in you for a reason. Make it a reality and you are giving back to the world so much more. Maybe your dream cures a disease or maybe it entertains people. Maybe you inspire someone else to chase their dream. Maybe it creates new jobs or it makes you money that you can tithe or donate to a cause. Maybe that money gives someone a new opportunity or maybe that money funds research to treat or cure cancer. Who knows what your dream can do for the world unless you go after it!

Barrier 3: External Influences

They think I am crazy/silly/going to fail . . .

We discussed internal feedback in the form of self-talk. Now it is time to discuss the external feedback we constantly receive. As we reach adulthood, the idea of having to deal with peer pressure seems trite and a concept that is only relevant in your formative years. Unfortunately, most of us have to be aware of "peer pressure" all our lives. No, I'm not talking about your friends that are taunting you to try your first cigarette or to take a sip of beer or skip class. This is much more subtle and can be just as powerful and maybe even more so.

It can come in the form of your parent's opinion of what is best for you as a teenager and show up several decades later when you are considering a career change. It can show up as your friends laughing at a business idea you were thinking about pursuing. It can be a caring coworker who is a natural pessimist and gets down on just about everything. It can even be something as big and vague as society's ideals. Whatever the source, it could be a large daunting barrier on your success journey, and without looking out for it, you may not even know it is getting in your way.

We will start with the ideals of society, as that is influencing so many others' perceptions. Society seems to encourage old, outdated ideas. Ideas such as a safe and secure nine-to-five job with benefits where you work most of your life. This work concept became outdated in the 1980–'90s, but as a society, apparently it takes a while to sink in. Society seems to think companies and governments are in business to take care of us. This simply allows the masses to pass responsibility of their own lives to large indefinite entities and makes it easy to wag our fingers at them. The ideals of society seem to loom over our heads shaping even our most impassioned ideas.

Now we can talk about everyone else: parents, friends, colleagues, relatives, etc. Each of them has had their beliefs shaped during their formative years and typically those beliefs are reinforced in adulthood. There are two types of advice and both are typically given with what is to be believed as your best interests in mind. It's not whether the advice is good or bad. It's not whether the advice is knowledgeable or not. It has everything to do with the spirit of the advice.

Is the advice you are being given drenched in fear, doubt, worry, concern, anxiety, and jealously or simply raw emotion? Then you are probably talking to a detractor. Another way to know this is they typically offer these opinions without hearing much more than a summary of an idea. If the advice feels factual, logical, caring, and done in a way that is centered in possibility thinking, then there is a good chance that person is sharing their thoughts with you in a supportive way. That is what you need. Don't get me wrong, they may give you a thousand pitfalls to consider and it may be tough news to swallow, and it may even change your mind about a course of action, but typically this person will position it in a supportive and relating way.

How do you deal with the detractors? As much as you might want to, you can't cut all the negative people out of your life. But there are a few things you can do. You can limit your exposure and what you share.

If it's a relative, just because you are related doesn't mean you have to tell them everything that is going on in your life. You can limit what you share to avoid the negative soap-boxing. Or, when your coworker gets on their soapbox about how your idea will never work, you take that feedback and you don't even let it in. I know you will be tempted to get into a debate and lay out your 100-point plan on how it will work exactly and what the top ten benefits are with an irresistible return on investment, but unless they are a decision maker of someone you need to sell your idea to, there is no point. They have likely already made their mind up for whatever reason.

Unfortunately, you will find chronically negative people and sometimes you just have to limit your exposure. And, even worse, you might find cruel, unsupportive people who take negativity to a near abusive or neglecting level. This isn't always a popular move but sometimes you need to cut those people out of your life, sometimes completely. I hope you don't have anyone in your life like this. If you do, you might want to seek the support of a professional counselor or therapist.

The best way to overcome those negative people is to surround yourself with positive people and possibility thinkers. I'm not talking about the eternal optimist who will tell you everything will be okay and then ride away on their unicorn. I'm talking about aligning with winners, entrepreneurs, progressive thinkers, movers and shakers, market disruptors, thought leaders, mentors, coaches—anyone and everyone who is striving forward. It's always a good idea to find those people who are looking to accomplish what you want to accomplish. I'm not talking about being BFFs with your potential competitor, but why not? That could happen and it happens all the time.

How do you find them? Odds are you know some already. You probably are drawn to them but are afraid to engage with them on their level because you have been conditioned not to. Talk to them. Ask them to grab coffee with you to "pick their brain." It doesn't sound pleasant, but people tend to like their brain being "picked."

Find or start a mastermind group. This is a group of forward moving people who help each other with their respective ideas. The time spent together as a mastermind group includes brainstorming, accountability, networking, education, etc. and is a great way to tap the ideas of several bright minds to aid you in your success journey.

Trade organizations, networking groups, and civic organizations are also a good place to find positive thinkers to interact with. (Just be warned that detractors and negative people can be found in those groups too, so you'll want to assess the connections you make there.)

Finally, there may be some diamonds in the rough who you already know that on the surface appear to be a detractor, but they are looking for some inspiration for them to break free and start a success journey of their own. Your journey may be the catalyst to get them started. You never know who you will inspire. As I mentioned earlier, the world needs you to pursue your dream.

Barrier 4: Life Constraints

I am too busy. I don't have any money, and I have no idea how to even start.

Life has a way of getting in the way of our dreams. There are so many things that might not align for you to begin your success journey. We hear a lot of reasons why others don't chase their dreams. Odds are you have used or are using some of these reasons as well:

Time – I know you are busy. I am busy, too. Everyone is busy. We are all so very busy. And, everyone is fighting for a piece of our time. It's so bad, the perception of "being busy" is now worn as a badge of honor, especially in the United States. People view "workaholism" as a good thing. There is something always going on.

For instance, take your family. There is always a birthday party to attend or a wedding or a holiday gathering, and not to mention your friends' activities. When is there time to pursue your dream? There isn't. There isn't any time to chase your dream and make it a reality, unless you realize there is.

It's tricky. It's a trade-off. You must make the time to chase this dream or it will never happen.

Time is your most valuable commodity. We can always make more money or learn new skills, but we can never get time back. We choose how to use a minute or an hour and once they are gone, we never get them back. So, you must constantly ask yourself: "Is this the best use of my time to achieve my dream and make the life I choose?"

If the answer is "yes," then there is a good chance it is. If the answer is "no," then you should probably pass on whatever it is. (Advice: sometimes something that doesn't appear to be obviously in your best interests for your dream may actually be in your best interest in the long term. Spending time with your spouse or visiting a friend, for example. After all, there are many reasons you are going on your success journey, you don't want to achieve your dream and be all alone. Don't create "dreamaholism" instead of "workaholism.")

Money – The great thing about today's world is things are so much more accessible and self-serving than in the past. There are so many ways now-a-days to circumnavigate things that traditionally cost money. Of course there are some things you absolutely need to spend money on, but that doesn't mean you need to go get an angel investor to make your dreams come true.

In fact the best ways to raise the money you need is to work harder in your current job, or to work extra, or maybe even take on some jobs that you normally wouldn't. But guess what? Even in those circumstances, you can turn those into learning experiences. Nothing else builds character like those experiences. There is nothing better in today's world by starting up in a garage or basement and creating something from near nothing. Some of our world's greatest success stories start with humble beginnings.

Earning to save is one way. Another way is cutting out expenses to save. Do you really need the premium cable package? Do you need your daily $5 latte? (I know this one will meet resistance as I am a voracious coffee drinker.) Do you need to order pizza twice a week? Do you need to eat out for lunch every day at the office? There are critical cuts you can make and they can add up fast.

Get creative to help fuel your endeavors. Bartering used to be very popular and it still works. You have skills and abilities that are unique to you. Quite possibly they are of value to others; and more importantly, it is possible these skills and abilities are of value to others that have or do what may be valuable to you on your success journey. Don't be afraid to suggest trading services.

Knowledge – This is probably the easiest IF you know what you need. A lot of people think they need way more knowledge than they do and shell out thousands of dollars for college courses or worse tens of thousands for a degree or two. Yes, sometimes you need those things. If you want to be a doctor of anything you will need to go through formal training at accredited universities. But if you are starting a photography business you probably don't need to wait to get a master›s degree. (I'm not saying don't ever get it, but typically it isn't something you need to wait to do first. Just like with many things it depends on your dream.)

The first step is to acknowledge what you already know and what you need to fulfill your dream. There are probably a lot of experiences in your life that transition well to what you are about to do.

You can find mentors in the area you wish to pursue and ask to pick their brains or even see if they are willing to help guide you through your endeavor. It is easier to connect with people who have done it before, who are willing to share their experiences and help you avoid the pitfalls and dead ends they may have experienced on their own journey. Also, you can find mentors through SCORE, an association supported by the Small Business Administration. These are volunteers who have succeeded in certain areas of business and agree to mentor and advise aspiring entrepreneurs and professionals.

There is also the Small Business Administration (SBA), which has programs, training, counseling, and assist with small business loans when applicable. This organization has a wealth of knowledge that is available to anyone.

We live in such an amazing time. It used to be that if you wanted to learn about something, you had to go down to the local university or community college and enroll in a course for several weeks and then get in your car or take the bus and show up once or twice a week whether it was raining, snowing, or the dark of night. Today, not only can we just hop on our computer and find a plethora of online training courses, but you can be sitting almost anywhere and connect with the same plethora of online training courses on your phone. Companies like Udemy have created a platform for experts to create courses which may in turn provide you with what you need to know.

In that same vein, there are a myriad of videos and presentations out there. Most of these videos and presentations have relevant and factual information and the vast majority of them are completely free with your account to any one of the big video sites. One word of caution is that while most of these sources are solid, knowledgeable, and reputable, there are some that may not have a clue what they are talking about. It is best to compare and contrast and take everything in with slight skepticism. The good news is as you learn and become more knowledgeable on a subject, you will be able to figure out quicker which sources are good and which are junk.

Another easy solution to solving a lack of knowledge barrier is sometimes to just hire or barter for the skillsets you need. If you are starting a business and you need a website as we all do now, then you could pick a do-it-yourself site and just do it yourself. Or you can just hire someone to do it for you and probably get it done quicker and better than if you would have done it; and it allows you the time to learn about the things you need to learn about.

Finally, a tried-and-true method to learning: read, read, read, and read some more. Abraham Lincoln said, "A capacity and taste for reading gives access to whatever has already been discovered by others." Or if you prefer something with a little more rhythm: "The more you read, the more things you will know. The more that you learn, the more places you'll go," from Dr. Seuss. You can take a big chunk out of any knowledge gap by thoroughly digesting a few solid books on any subject. It probably won't give you everything you need, but it can speed you in the right direction.

Experience – First, look at your transferable experience from past jobs that are relevant and similar to what you need on your success journey. Don't just disregard everything you have done in the past. Odds are there are some real gems of experience that you can point to as relevant experience.

Don't be afraid to pilot and test some things to gain experience and at the same time test market an idea/product/service, etc. If it fits what your dream is, even giving away services for a testimonial might be a good way to get experience. Other dreams might not allow for that type of opportunity, so another way is to try to get as much exposure as possible in the form of practical observation, special projects, extra credit, published articles, etc. Just go above and beyond and soak it all in. Another way is to volunteer your services or products or ideas to non-profit organizations. You won't make money, but there isn't a better and more fulfilling way to get experience than to give back even as you are getting started. It doesn't get much better than that. There are lots of ways to overcome the lack of experience barrier. The best thing is to just dive in.

Barrier 5: Waiting for Permission
I don't know if I am ready.

Throughout my life I have noticed an underlying theme with a lot of people. Many of us act as if we need permission to do things. As children, yes of course, this is a good practice. We need permission to go places, buy things, watch things, etc. This practice serves us well. It is intended to keep us safe and on the right path.

But the problem is as we grow older, we still seek permission. Young adults seek their parents' approval as they go to college or enter the workforce. Or they look to ask permission of authority figures to make decisions on their behalf. Some people continue to seek permission from family, spouses, bosses, colleagues, clergy, etc. all of their lives. They wait for someone to tell them they can move forward with a dream and a lot of the times they just keep their dream to themselves.

There are a lot of memes going around the internet these days that say "If you are waiting for a sign, this is it." Some are funny, some are inspirational, but they are out there to tell the reader to stop waiting for permission and to get moving.

Only you need to give you permission. You are the only one who can do any of the things we discussed earlier. If you really truly need someone to actually give you permission; if you still struggle with this notion and need someone's approval to move forward, then let Sean and I give you that permission right now. **From this moment on, you have Sean's and my permission to move forward on your own success journey to achieve your dream. We support you.** In fact, there are many others reading this book who will support you and give you permission to proceed, too.

Some final thoughts on barriers. We all face these barriers from time to time. Some of us face all of them, some of us face one or two of them, some of us have overcome these barriers and need to remain vigilant of them. It is okay to have these challenges and it is okay to need to face these before you are able to move forward. Sometimes these barriers may be too much for you to handle on your own or there may be other barriers standing in your way that require professional assistance.

I always think it is a good idea to seek the help of a professional therapist even if you don't feel like you are facing any challenges, let alone if you are experiencing any challenges. These professionals help you understand yourself and help you relate to the world around you. Please take the time to consider talking to a professional if some of these barriers feel too tall to take on alone.

Chapter 13
Start at the End and
Work Backwards

You just faced several barriers that might have blocked your way during this most important step of your success journey. You are now going to see yourself at the end of your success journey having achieved your dream.

We are going to begin by defining your dream. We need to add as much detail as we possibly can. We need to add so much rich texture and meaning, that in your mind's eye it is as real as it is going to actually be.

Consider this statement: "I want a million dollars." What do you think your odds for success are if you just say that? How about "I want to open a restaurant."? That is slightly better because it says at least what you are going to do. What about "I will open a restaurant and that will make me a million dollars."? Closer.

"I will open the most successful authentic Nepalese restaurant in Pittsburgh, Pennsylvania on Pittsburgh's North Shore by May 1, 2017. It will be a bright modern dining space with an open-kitchen. On my menu, I will serve dal bhat and yak burgers. When I walk in, I can hear the sizzle of the yak being prepared in the kitchen and I can smell the spicy aroma of the select seasonings we use to prepare our food. Over the bar will be a realistic replica of the biggest shaggiest yak head you've ever seen…" I think you are getting the point. It needs rich textured detail. Let's start collecting that detail!

Before you start answering my questions, you will want a pen and paper; you are going to write this all down. Mark Twain said, "The dullest pencil is better than the sharpest mind." You will want to capture this all down and refer back to it. Now let's begin:

1. Find a quiet place to sit, think and write. Do your best to find a location that best helps you concentrate and think. Go out on a patio, find a picnic table, find a window with a view, or a window without a view. If you are in a crowded coffee shop or on a plane, pop on those headphones and put in some type of inspiring background music. You know you best.

2. Once you are in your quiet place, you are going to take a first pass at your dream by simply answering the question: "What is your dream?" I know it's heavy to go straight into it. It doesn't have to be detailed yet. It can just be a sentence or a statement or even a word. "Chef," "Pediatrician," or "Architect" are all a good start.

3. Stop and answer this question: Is this what you want? It's not your spouse's idea or your parents' influence. Is this dream 100 percent your own desire? Will it make you happy?

4. Then answer this question: Is what you are going to do legal, moral, and ethical? The world doesn't need more bank robberies or affairs. The world needs the realization of good dreams with substance and purpose.

5. Now answer this: "What does success look like for you?" Take the time to imagine and then write down what it would look like to be successful in this dream of yours. Allow yourself some time to answer this question.

6. Consider what you have so far. What does that look like? Do you have detail? Are you excited about what you wrote or did it feel like a school assignment? Regardless of the answer you are going to spend some time with your dream and in great detail. You want so much detail that you begin to imagine it as real—so real that you even start to smell it.

7. We are going to add even more detail to what you have. This is your dream and you have permission to dream big and dream deep.

Here are several questions to help you:

- What does your daily activity look like?
- Do you have a business title?
- What city or town do you live in?
- What does your house look like?

- How do you interact with loved ones?
- How do you interact with everyone else?
- How is your health?
- What activities do you pursue for fun?
- Do you have pets? What types? What are their names?
- Where do you vacation?

And, keep going...what else can you add? What kind of car do you drive? Do you fly first class now? Does your favorite restaurant have your favorite table reserved for you for every visit?

- Now that you have a foundation for your dream, it is time to add meaning. You are going to imagine yourself being successful in your dream and take the time to answer the following questions and write down how you feel about it.
- What does it mean to you?
- How much have you changed along the journey?
- What does this mean to your life?
- Who are you serving by achieving your dream?
- What does this mean to them?
- Are you giving back to your church, charities, those in need, etc.?
- Are you inspiring others in your life just by living your dream?

Keep going! This is your "why." This is the "Why" that makes the achievement of your dream so much more important than just a goal written on a piece of paper. This is what is going to get you through many of the challenges you may face and keep you focused on your dream.

- What is riding on your dream?
- Is it for personal satisfaction?
- Do you have a family to support?
- Is it to bring hope to children that have been touched by cancer?

Write down what brings out the emotion in you and connect it to your dream.

Ignore any resistance to being thorough and creative because you might not know exactly what it is going looks like in many ways. Be creative to fill in any blanks. That is the point! You are only limited by your own imagination!

Here is your last instruction to this part of the exercise: HAVE FUN WITH IT! Laugh a little, smile, happy-cry, get emotionally attached to the meaning of your dream. But spend time with this. This is a big deal! You will change your life!

Consider for a moment Sean's dream of climbing Mt. Everest and being the first cancer survivor to do so and even with one lung! What did that mean to his life? It meant he could travel the world and inspire countless people to achieve their dreams. It meant he could visit children with cancer in hospitals all over the world and give them hope. It meant he could continue to inspire people by climbing the Seven Summits and do it for everyone who has ever been touched by cancer.

Now that you have this all written down. It's time to write your dream statement.

Crafting Your Dream Statement

You have spent some time writing down what your dream will look like. Not only do you have what you will be doing, but also why you are doing it. Let's now craft a clear statement that you can use to serve as your focus when you imagine achieving your dream. This is what you will use to help see yourself as successful at the end of your success journey just as Sean saw himself already on the summit of Mt. Everest!

I am going to walk you through the crafting of your dream statement step by step:

1. Begin with "I am." The words "I am" are so powerful. Whatever you put after those two words defines you. "I am tired" just zaps the energy out of you when you say it. For fun, blurt out loud, "I am the greatest!" How did that feel? Pretty good, huh? Starting with "I am" makes it a part of you. It is the most important step in creating your dream statement.

2. Your dream statement must be in the present tense. You want to see yourself in the moment that you complete your success journey. Sean wasn't seeing himself wanting to climb a mountain, he saw himself already on the summit of the highest mountain in the world. Your mind will believe that you are already successful.

3. Give your dream statement a concrete specific date to complete it by. This includes day, month, and year. Simply stating "in one year I am on the top of Mt. Everest" isn't going to do it because each day you think about your dream, it is exactly a year from that particular day. Using phrases such

as "a year from today," "a year from tomorrow," or "a year from the day after tomorrow" will only allow your mind will see it as getting pushed out daily. But, if it has a solid date assigned to it, then on every day the mind is working to manifest it in the timeframe provided.

4. Include all of your senses, if you can. This not only will help provide vivid imagery, but will help you with your visualization. Sean's example reads something like this: "As I stand on the summit of Mt. Everest, I see mountain peaks poking through a sea of clouds. I can hear the hard snow crunch under my boot. I feel the cold wind whipping across my face, and I can smell the air rich with ozone." Engaging all of your senses makes it even more real in your mind.

5. And, now for the great differentiator, after you have owned it with "I am" and see yourself as having completed it with a specific date, you want to state what it means to you and others. Sean constantly reminded himself why he was climbing Mt. Everest. He was doing it for everyone on Earth that has ever been touched by cancer. That was his fuel. This was not only for him but for so many others. He used this as his driving force even when things seemed their darkest.

Take the time to craft your dream statement and allow yourself to feel the meaning behind what you are doing. Write it down on an index card, journal, app, or whatever you prefer that you can keep with you to quickly reference it. It becomes more real when it's written down.

The Dream Statement Checklist

Let's check your dream statement. With so many key pieces of equipment and items to check on, one can imagine how important a checklist is to any explorer. In Kathmandu, before Sean was ready to travel to Base Camp, experienced Sherpas took the time to review his gear to ensure Sean had everything he needed to make the journey and the summit. Missing any one of these essential items could spell disaster.

Now that you have crafted your dream statement, let's double check your dream statement with a checklist of your own. This is your Dream Statement Checklist. It may not necessarily spell disaster in your quest to achieve your dream, but by having all of these key components accounted for, it will increase your chances of success.

Checklist for crafting your best dream statement:

- Is it your own dream?
- Is what you want moral and ethical?
- Do you own it with "I am"?
- Is it written in the present tense?
- Is there a clear deadline? (Month, Day, Year, even Time!)
- Have you included multiple senses?
- Have you included meaning that elicits feelings from you?
- Is it on a card, journal, app, etc. that you can consistently keep with you to looks at often?

If you checked each of these off, then CONGRATULATIONS! You have crafted your dream statement. You are now ready to embark on your success journey!

The Next Step on Your Success Journey

Now that you have crafted your dream statement, the next step on your success journey is to create a few new habits:

1. Put yourself in a relaxed state.
2. Review your dream statement at least twice per day every day.
3. Imagine having successfully achieving your dream at least twice per day, every day.

The best time to review your dream statement and imagine achieving your dream is in the first thirty minutes of waking. First, find a quiet place and read your dream statement out loud if you can. Take some time to get into a relaxed state of mind by doing some progressive relaxations exercises. You can use what Sean referenced in his story and systematically tense all the muscles in your body from head to toe and slowly release them and do this ten times. Or, meditate or do some light yoga. Choose whatever works best for you in order to enter a relaxed state.

Next, take the next ten minutes to imagine yourself having successfully completed your success journey with all that vivid detail you wrote down in an earlier exercise. It may be challenging at first, but like every exercise you will begin to develop visualization muscles and eventually you will be able to slip into your visualization easily.

If you need to reference the detail you wrote down in the earlier exercise, please do so. Imagine the detail and feel the meaning. See in your mind's eye what it means to you personally and even what it means to others. Imagine with all of your senses. What do you see, hear, feel, smell, and taste? Sense it all!

Then right before you go to sleep, repeat the above exercise. Do this every day. This is your new habit and the first summit of success climbed in your own success journey.

Sometimes people have a hard time seeing some of those things in their mind and imagining with all of their senses. If you are one of them, you might want to get pictures to help. Post them on a bulletin board or poster board where you can quickly reference them if you need to. There are apps that allow you to this on your phone or computer and those are okay, but you want the visual of it up and in front of you.

I'm a big fan of being paperless. However, I still put things on my wall for reference. In fact, I have a large and long sheet of paper on my wall mapping this and future books out so that I can quickly reference it and be inspired by it. It keeps me on track and incites the emotion of doing something grand that can positively impact so many people.

You can also find music or sounds that might help trigger your visualization as well as smells. Have you ever had a nostalgic feeling when you smell a certain fragrance? How about those people that enjoy that "new car smell?" Smell can be equally powerful. Find sounds and scents that can help you with your visualization in addition to visual aids.

In addition to these two new habits, if there are barriers that you need to overcome, you will want to take the steps to form some new habits for those as well. Some of these will be easy to change and you will quickly move on, but some of those barriers may follow you on your journey. You will have to continue forward and resist the urge to succumb to that barrier.

Finally, go to the *Inspiring Others: Reaching Your Personal Summit Facebook Page* and post your dream statement! Tell us what you will do, or rather; tell us what you did in the future. Let us and others support your dream. After the final book of the series, we will want to hear about your completed success journey. Share it with the world! We'll celebrate your success!

"Everest—a name synonymous with majesty, mystery, and greatness . . . but also with misery and death."

Your dream should evoke images and feelings equally intense, but now it's different. You can see yourself as having already completed your success journey. You are standing on your own summit of success.

You defined your dream. You can see your dream. Now practice seeing your dream daily.

Looking Ahead . . .
The Second Summit
to Your Success

As you work through what you learned in this book, create your new habits, and see yourself achieving your dream, we want to provide you a look at the next book and the next step on your success journey.

In the second book, Sean will take you on his first climb of Mt. Kilimanjaro and we will dig deeper into who you are. Our objectives in that book will be to understand and take stock of:

How you are wired.

How you interact with others.

Assess your skills and knowledge.

Assess areas of skill and knowledge opportunities.

Enjoy your success journey and start living your unstoppable life!

Continue the Conversation

Website: SeanSwarner.com
Email: Summit@SeanSwarner.com

About the Author

Sean Swarner is a philanthropist, author, and keynote speaker. He is a two-time terminal-cancer survivor who has dedicated his life to helping others reach their full potential.

Sean created Cancer Climber with his brother in 2001, a nonprofit organization that pays for and travels with cancer survivors to climb Kilimanjaro. Sean's passion for climbing and adventure blossomed after becoming the first cancer survivor to summit Mount Everest. Since then, he has climbed all seven summits and has skied to both North and South Poles, making him the first cancer survivor to complete the Explorers Grand Slam. He accomplished all of this and completed the Hawaii Ironman all while having only one functioning lung. His adventures and passions have captured the attention of millions, and in 2017, a team followed Sean to the North Pole and made a documentary about him and his triumphs. The documentary, *True North*, was released on Amazon Prime. In 2018, Sean was voted one of the Top 8 Most Inspirational People in history and was the recipient of the Don't Ever Give Up Award, presented by the Jimmy V Foundation and ESPN.

He splits his time between Colorado and Puerto Rico with his wife.

A free ebook edition is available with the purchase of this book.

To claim your free ebook edition:

1. Visit MorganJamesBOGO.com
2. Sign your name CLEARLY in the space
3. Complete the form and submit a photo of the entire copyright page
4. You or your friend can download the ebook to your preferred device

Morgan James BOGO™

A **FREE** ebook edition is available for you or a friend with the purchase of this print book.

CLEARLY SIGN YOUR NAME ABOVE

Instructions to claim your free ebook edition:
1. Visit MorganJamesBOGO.com
2. Sign your name CLEARLY in the space above
3. Complete the form and submit a photo of this entire page
4. You or your friend can download the ebook to your preferred device

Print & Digital Together Forever.

Snap a photo

Free ebook

Read anywhere

CPSIA information can be obtained
at www.ICGtesting.com
Printed in the USA
JSHW031940270122
22306JS00004B/469